SAVINGS

AND INVESTMENTS

Leo Gough

TEACH YOURSELF BOOKS

British Library Cataloguing in Publication Data

Gough, Leo
Savings and Investments. – (Teach yourself)
1. Finance, Personal
I. Title
332'.024

ISBN 0 340 67002-9

First published 1996
Impression number   10 9 8 7 6 5 4 3 2 1
Year   2000 1999 1998 1997 1996

Typeset by Transet Limited, Coventry, England.
Printed in Great Britain for Hodder & Stoughton Educational, a division of
Hodder Headline Plc, 338 Euston Road, London NW1 3BH by Cox & Wyman,
Reading, Berks.

CONTENTS

1

KEY CONCEPTS IN INVESTMENT

In this chapter we will look at:

- What saving and investment really mean
- Interest
- Inflation
- Liquidity
- Volatility
- Risk
- Comparing investments

What saving and investment really mean

A self-made multi-millionaire I know has a favourite saying: 'The way to have money is not to make it, or to spend it, but to save it.' It's the kind of aphorism you might expect from an elderly person on a low income, yet here is a middle-aged man who takes enormous business risks and spends more money on living expenses in one year than most people do in five, telling everyone he meets to save their money. What can he mean by it?

Like most worthwhile things in life, it is very simple. Saving just means putting aside money from your income and keeping it. The size of your income and the proportion of it that you save are irrelevant to the basic principle expressed in my millionaire friend's saying, that if you save money regularly, you will get richer.

Investment is, at root, an equally simple idea. Once you have saved money you can put it to work and make it grow faster. There are many ways of doing this, and in this book we will examine a number of tried and tested investment methods.

Both saving and investment are intimately related to time. To understand them properly, you have to think about how much time you have available. Once again, the answer is simple – you have the rest of your life in which to save and invest, however old you are now. As you pass through different life stages you will have different needs and your investment tactics will change (this is discussed in Chapter 2), but for now try to get into the habit of thinking of saving and investment as things you will do all your life, on a par with eating, brushing your teeth and washing.

Interest

There are many ways to save, but most people start by putting aside a proportion of the cash they receive as wages. You could simply put this money under the bed, but then it is 'dead' money – it won't grow, and it may well lose some of its buying power through inflation. Saving 'dead' money is better than not saving at all, but you can make it 'live' and grow by putting it somewhere where it will earn interest.

'Interest' is a fee that someone will pay you if you lend them money for a period of time. If you borrow money from a bank you will have to pay the bank some interest, and if you put money in an interest-bearing account in, say, a bank, it will pay you interest in return for being able to use the money you have deposited.

Interest is usually expressed as an annual percentage of the money that is lent. Thus, if you deposit £100 in a building society which is offering 5% interest per annum (per year), at the end of the year you will have £105 in the account. If you are a taxpayer you will have to pay tax on the interest you earn, so the 'gross' rate of 5% will be reduced to, say, 3.75%.

Compound interest

If you leave your £100 in an account for several years you will accumulate several years' worth of interest, paid at set times during the period. As long as you leave it in the account, the interest you get will earn interest as well. This effect is known as 'compounding', and, while it doesn't seem very important in the short term, over many years it dramatically improves the rate of growth of your money.

EXAMPLE

Nicole puts £10,000 into an interest-bearing account which gives her 10% a year. For the sake of simplicity let's assume that the interest is paid at the end of each year and that she is only allowed to withdraw money at that point. After the first year her account look like this:

Year 1

Deposit	£10,000
10% interest	£1,000
Total	£11,000

After the second year her account looks like this:

Year 2

Deposit	£10,000
First year's interest	£1,000
Second year's interest	£1,000
10% interest on first year's interest	£100
Total	£12,100

Nicole has received an extra £100 pounds through the effect of compounding. If she leaves the money in the account for seven years, her initial deposit will have doubled to approximately £20,000, about £3,000 more than if she had taken the interest out of the account each time it was paid. Compounding is very important in saving and investment, particularly in the stock market, as we will see in Chapter 3.

There is a formula you can use to work out how money will compound which we will look at later in this chapter. It's more important, though, to know the rough and ready compounding rule known as the 'rule of 72'.

The rule of 72

This is simply a rough way of working out how long it will take for a sum of money to double through compounding at a given rate of interest. You just divide 72 by the annual interest rate.

EXAMPLE

Nicole is considering investing £10,000 in a scheme which, she thinks, will generate an average annual return of between 4% and 15%. Using the rule of 72 she works out that:

- at 4% her money will take about 72 ÷ 4 = 18 years to double
- at 10% her money will take about 72 ÷ 10 = 7.2 years to double
- at 15% her money will take about 72 ÷ 15 = 4.8 years to double

---

These calculations give her an idea of the range of possible returns she might get by investing.

The rule of 115

If you want to know roughly how long it will take for a sum of money to treble at a given rate of interest, simply divide 115 by the interest rate.

EXAMPLE

Nicole decides to apply the rule of 115 to her investment project:
- at 4% her money will take about 115 ÷ 4 = 28.75 years to treble
- at 10% her money will take about 115 ÷ 10 = 11.5 years to treble
- at 15% her money will take about 115 ÷ 15 = 7.6 years to treble

---

Notice that the longer she leaves her money in the investment, the more rapidly it grows because compounding makes the growth rate accelerate.

Inflation

Inflation is a phenomenon which complicates matters. Economists don't agree on exactly what causes it, but it can be defined as the lessening of the buying power of a sum of money over time.

EXAMPLE

Nicole puts £10,000 under the bed for a year in which the inflation rate is 10%. At the end of the year she still has £10,000, but it will buy, overall, 10% fewer goods and services than it could have done at the beginning of the year.

Initial sum	£10,000
Less 10% inflation	£1,000
Buying power	£9,000

Printing money

One of the causes of inflation is the printing of extra money by the authorities. This technique has been used for millennia, and is, in effect, the diluting of the value of currency by the issuing authorities.

EXAMPLE

The King of Ruritania has notes and coins in circulation to the value of 10 billion Ruritanian crowns. The Ruritanian people use this money in their daily lives. The King needs to raise 1 billion Ruritanian crowns to pay for some new roads. He doesn't want to borrow it, because he will have to pay interest, and he doesn't want to increase taxes because the people will complain, so he decides to print more money. The Ruritanian central bank secretly prints notes worth 1 billion Ruritanian crowns, and over the course of a few months the King dribbles this money out into the country by paying the road-building costs with it.

After a while, the sharper Ruritanian business people notice that there seems to be more cash around, particularly amongst the road-builders, so they raise their prices. Over a few months prices rise by 10%, so a Ruritanian crown now buys 10% less than it did before the King printed the extra money. The King knew this would happen, but he decided that it was worth it in order to get his roads built.

The Retail Prices Index (RPI)

Inflation is unpredictable in the medium to long term. In addition, it is not really possible to measure inflation exactly. Everyone, including the banks and the government, does need some way of measuring the rate of inflation, however, and one of the most commonly used indices is the Retail Prices Index (RPI).

The Retail Prices Index measures how much the prices of a group of goods and services have increased in a given period of time. The goods and services used are chosen to represent what an 'average' family spends its money on, and are 'weighted' to reflect the relative amounts of each item that the average family buys. It is only an approximation, so the actual inflation in the price of any particular item may be different from the RPI rate.

EXAMPLE

Nicole is a commercial artist who spends about £3,000 a year on acrylic paints. The RPI in a particular year increases by 5%, so she assumes that she has spent 5% more on acrylic paints in the previous year than she did in the year before. Five per cent of £3,000 is £150, so when she comes to do her accounts she expects to find that she has spent £3,150 on paint, but she actually finds that she has spent £3,300 for the same amount of paint as she has bought in previous years. Acrylic paint has cost her 10% more than in previous years, so although the RPI tells her that inflation has gone up by 5%, paint prices have actually inflated by 10%.

The RPI is a very useful measure of inflation, but it does not tell you exactly what rates of increase you are experiencing in the prices of the things you actually buy yourself.

The real rate of return

Investors know that inflation will reduce the buying power of their money over time, and that interest rates go up and down to reflect this. Broadly speaking, when inflation is high, interest rates will be high, and when inflation is low, interest rates will be low. Interest rates and inflation are not locked together, however, so it sometimes happens that the interest rate you can get from a bank deposit is actually less than the rate of inflation.

At the time of writing (summer 1996) inflation has been low for several years. Most people think that low inflation is a good thing, because it makes it easier to plan financially. Mortgage rates, for example, are lower than they have been for decades and it is easy to borrow at a fixed interest rate in order to buy a house. There is no reason to believe, however, that inflation will remain low for many years to come. If it starts to rise, the cost of borrowing will rise with it.

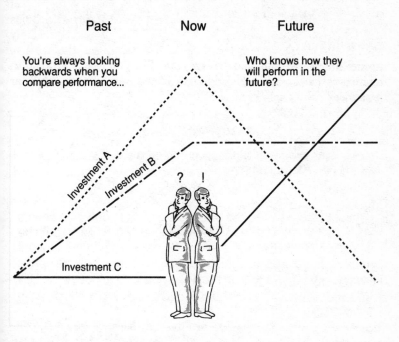

Figure 1.1 No-one can predict the future with total accuracy

Uncertainty about inflation causes investors to switch their investments around more than they might do otherwise. At times when inflation is high, investors don't like to have much cash, and they tend to put their money into things which will keep pace with, or beat, the inflation rate. Historically, house prices have beaten inflation when inflation has been high. When inflation is low, investors tend to take their money out of things such as houses, and keep more of it in cash.

When you assess the return (which means the reward) that you may get from any particular investment, you need to take inflation into account. What you really need to know is the 'real rate of return' you will get, after you have accounted for inflation. This is all based on estimates when you are looking ahead, since no-one knows exactly what will happen in the future; you will only know your real rate of return with hindsight.

As a general rule of thumb, if you get a 5% overall real rate of return on your investments in the long term you are doing reasonably well. This does not include running a business, which is riskier than most types of investing but may give better returns.

A rough way of working out the real rate of return is to subtract the inflation rate from the interest rate, or growth rate, you get from an investment.

EXAMPLE

In one year, Nicole gets 10% interest on a deposit of £10,000, but the RPI has gone up by 8%.

Deposit	£10,000
Interest	£1,000

At the end of the year she has £11,000, but the buying power of the money has reduced by 8%, so:

8% of 11,000 = 880
11,000 − 880 = 10,120

Nicole could say that her real return has only been 2%, or £200. This is imprecise because of the effect of compounding, but it is near enough to tell her that her real rate of return has been fairly low.

In fact, cash deposits do usually generate low real rates of return, as we will see in Chapter 4.

Liquidity

This brings us to the very important concept of liquidity, which many people do not really understand. If you can grasp liquidity, you are well on the way to becoming a skilled investor.

Imagine that all things of value are made of liquid. Here are some examples, in descending order of liquidity.

- Cash is the most 'runny' of all these things – you can draw it out of the bank and spend it whenever you want.
- A cheque isn't quite as 'runny', since you have to deposit it in a bank and wait three days for it to clear.
- There are things like good quality stocks and shares which can be sold by telephoning your broker – you get the money in a few days.
- If you know what you are doing when you buy and sell second-hand furniture, you will find that some items can be sold fairly fast – say within a month or so.
- Houses aren't very 'runny' at all. They are more 'runny' during a housing boom, and less 'runny' when the market is slow, but at any time they take longer to sell than the items mentioned above.

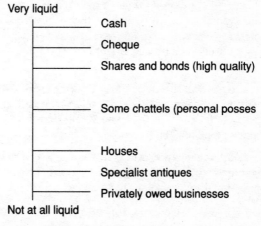

Very liquid

Cash
Cheque
Shares and bonds (high quality)

Some chattels (personal posses

Houses
Specialist antiques
Privately owed businesses

Not at all liquid

Figure 1.2 The relative liquidity of various forms of investment.

You have to put the house on the market, wait for people to come and see it, go through the palaver of negotiating the price, wait for all the conveyancing and financing procedures to be concluded, and then, finally, you get your money. This process can take months, if not years.

● Some specialist items are even less liquid than houses. Examples include shares in a private business, and rare antiques. These can take years to sell; you can sell them more quickly if you are willing to take a substantial loss, but if you want a fair price you may have to do a lot of work over a long period of time.

Liquidity is a way of describing how easily and quickly something can be sold. High liquidity is valuable, because it gives you the chance to change your mind. Low liquidity, or 'illiquidity', is less valuable because you are stuck with the asset until you can sell it.

Most of the stories you hear about people making fortunes are actually about dealings in illiquid assets. Since illiquidity is unpopular, someone with luck and judgement can make large profits by buying at a low price and selling at a high price. This is much harder to do with highly liquid assets because everybody know what they are worth.

Volatility

Volatility means how rapidly the price of something goes up and down. You only really know how volatile something is in hindsight – for example, you can look at the performance of a particular stock market over a number of years and say that prices were volatile during that period, but you cannot be certain how volatile it will be in the future.

The more volatile things are, the harder it is to plan. Suppose that you never knew whether the price of bread in your local shop was going to be £5.00 or 5p – you would find it very hard to control your weekly food budget.

You can make quick profits in volatile investments by buying low and selling high, but, in general, this will be more by luck than good judgement unless you are an insider.

Risk

These days much investment literature has to carry a 'wealth warning', which is a statement along the lines that the prices of stocks and shares can go down as well as up, and that before deciding to invest you should seek financial and tax advice. One might think that nobody in their right minds could have thought otherwise, but 'wealth warnings' do have a useful function; it can be easy to get so excited about the details of an investment that you forget to consider what might happen if you lost money.

The amount of risk you take is usually, but not always, closely linked to the size of the return you may make.

One of the great arts of investment is the analysis of risk, and we will look at some theories of risk below. Before doing so, we should examine some important points about risk:

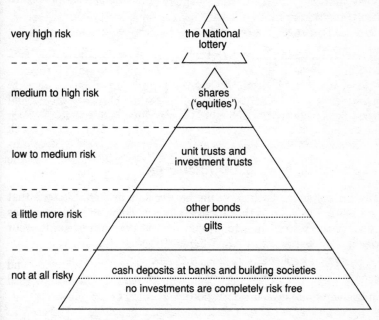

very high risk — the National lottery

medium to high risk — shares ('equities')

low to medium risk — unit trusts and investment trusts

a little more risk — other bonds / gilts

not at all risky — cash deposits at banks and building societies / no investments are completely risk free

Figure 1.3 How risky are investments?

- diversification
- there is no such thing as zero risk
- 'trees don't grow up to the sky'

Diversification

Diversification means not putting all your eggs in one basket. By spreading your wealth amongst different assets you reduce risk to some degree because if a disaster happens to one 'basket' of assets, the others may escape. Figure 1.3 shows a scale of the relative risk of different types of asset.

There is no such thing as zero risk

There really isn't! If there were a nuclear war, or a terrible plague, all bets would be off! Sitting at home at your desk, you might say that there is zero risk of being struck by lightning or killed by an earthquake, but you would be wrong – there is a tiny change that such things might happen. So it is with investments; even the most copperbottomed, gilt-edged guarantee does not assure you of zero risk.

This fact is nothing to worry about, however. It is part of life, and most of us instinctively know that it is the case. It is helpful, though, occasionally to consider all the bad things that might happen to your investments – it helps you to develop the cold, shrewd eyes that investors need to see through all the blarney that is talked and written about money.

'Trees don't grow up to the sky'

This famous saying is often applied to investments in rapidly growing companies. The point is that there are limits to how far anything will grow. Just as a tree will stop growing higher after a number of years, so will a company. If this didn't happen, then all the business in the world would be controlled by one single company which had absorbed all the others and kept on growing!

From the private investor's perspective, it is important to realise that during rapid periods of growth in a market it seems as if that growth will never end. Think of the boom in the housing market in the late 1980s – if you said that house prices might drop you were laughed at. In the same way, you may have an investment in the shares of a company which is growing dramatically; it is hard to believe that the growth will ever slow or stop, but it will. One member of the famous Rothschild family said, 'I made my fortune by selling too soon', meaning that he sold investments before their prices dropped.

EXAMPLE

John bought £1,000 pounds' worth of shares in Polly Peck plc in 1980 and decided to hold them for the long term. By the spring of 1990, John's shares are worth £1,300,000 – an astonishingly good result. Despite negative rumours about the company, John decides to hold on to the shares. After all, he reasons, there have been bad rumours about the company before.

Then John's wife Sarah persuades him to sell £300,000 pounds' worth of shares in order to buy a house. He has to pay some capital gains tax on this money, and only sells with great reluctance.

Then, at the end of 1990, the company is put into administration and its founder is the subject of criminal charges. John's shares are virtually worthless and unsaleable. He is inconsolable. 'I was a millionaire,' he wails, 'and now it's all gone.' Sarah has more sense. 'We still have the house, you twit,' she smiles.

Modern portfolio theory (MPT)

MPT was invented in the 1950s by Harry Markowitz, an American investment genius. It describes a way of investing in a collection of assets (a 'portfolio') in such a way as to make the collection less risky than any one of the assets within it. The mathematics of MPT are extremely complicated, but you can understand the principle by considering the next example.

EXAMPLE

Suppose you live in an isolated country that has only two businesses, a soft drink manufacturer and a raincoat manufacturer. In this country on average it is cold and rainy half the time and very hot and sunny for the other half of the time. In any particular year, however, nobody knows how much rain or sun there will be.

John puts £100 into the raincoat company and £100 into the soft drink company, knowing that when it is sunny, the soft drink company does well, and when it is rainy the raincoat company does well.
After 8 years he looks at his real returns:

Weather	Raincoats %	Drinks %	
Sunny	-30	60	
Rainy	60	-30	
Rainy	60	-30	
Rainy	60	-30	
Rainy	60	-30	
Sunny	-30	60	
Rainy	60	-30	
Rainy	60	-30	
Total:	300	-60	=240

John has lost £60 on the soft drinks investment, but he has made £300 on the raincoat maker, giving him an overall return

If John had invested all of the £200 in raincoats he would have made £300. If he had put the whole £200 in soft drinks he would have lost £120 of his capital, leaving him with only £80 to reinvest. If he had done this, it would take him a long time to build the £80 back up to the original level, and he might make more losses. This illustrates the strong argument for diversifying.

Technically, the two companies in the example have negative covariance, which means that when one does well the other doesn't. In real life, investments rarely have perfect negative covariance – if they did, you would be on to a 'sure thing', and it should be plain by now that there is no such thing as a sure thing in investment. What MPT does is to help you find investments which have low or negative covariance so that you can reduce your risk by diversifying.

Comparing investments

You don't have to be a mathematical genius to do well at investing, but it does help to be able to perform some calculations from time to time, particularly if you are trying to make your mind up about which of a number of investments you should choose. In this section we will look at some useful calculations.

- Present value and future value
- Working out a future value

Present value and future value

On page 8 we looked at the calculation of interest using the examples of Nicole, who put £10,000 into an account giving her 10% interest a year. The £10,000 she invested at the beginning is called the 'present value' (PV) and the total that she will have at the end of a specified period is called the 'future value' (FV), so the future value after one year will be £11,000.

Working out a future value

To work out the future value of a stream of payments, for example when you are saving a regular amount, use the formula:

$$FV = [p \times < (1 + i)^n - 1>] \div i$$

where p is the amount invested per period, n is the number of periods and i is the rate of interest per period.

EXAMPLE

Nicole wants to save £1,000 a year in an investment which she expects to generate a rate of interest of 7% a year. She wants to hold the investment for 12 years. To work out the future value, she uses the formula:

$$FV = [p \times <(1 + i)^n - 1>] / 1$$

$$
\begin{aligned}
FV &= [1{,}000 \times <(1 + 0.07)^{12} - 1>] / 0.07 \\
&= [1{,}000 \times <1.07^{12} - 1>] / 0.07 \\
&= [1{,}000 \times <1.07^{12} - 1>] / 0.07 \\
&= [1{,}000 \times <2.2522 - 1>] / 0.07 \\
&= [1{,}000 \times 1.2522] / 0.07 \\
&= 1252.20 / 0.07 \\
&= 17{,}888.57
\end{aligned}
$$

Thus although Nicole will only have put in a total of £12,000 over 12 years, at the end of the period she will have accumulated £17,888.57.

Conclusion

The ideas presented above will take time to sink in, so go over this chapter every so often to remind yourself of them. Remember that you have the rest of your life in which to develop your investment skills, so learn at your own pace. If you want to go further into the mathematics of investment, see the Bibliography for some useful books.

2

YOUR LIFE PLAN

Saving and investment are an art as well as a science, and it is up to each individual to decide how to integrate them into their lives. By giving some thought to the future course of your life and identifying your main priorities you will be able to make sensible decisions about your money more easily.

In this chapter we will look at:

- Life stages and how they affect investment
- The medium-term effects of divorce, job loss and children
- Investing in the short, medium and long-term
- Reviewing your current circumstances
- Calculating your net worth
- Investment and personality

Life stages and how they affect investment

As you move through the different stages of adult life your needs and abilities will change. While there are many imponderables, such as not knowing how long you will live, how many children you will have or whether you will remain healthy all your life, it is still possible to outline broad stages of development which most people go through.

Such a categorisation may disturb you if, like me, you are wary of generalisations. After all, you may say, what if I make a million and retire at the age of 30? Does this mean that I miss some of the stages? The point is really that human beings are all subject to the same broad physical limitations – there are only a certain number of years in which a human body can reproduce, for example, and human bodies are not usually as vigorous in old age as they are when they are young. The four categories listed below are simply a way of looking at how biological realities affect our financial lives, and introduce a degree of predictability, which is always helpful in investment planning.

Stage 1 Early adulthood – the twenties

In your twenties you have a lot of energy but not much experience. You are still shaping yourself as a person and still exploring wide career possibilities. It is a great time for spending, and people at this stage rarely want to save for the long term; the priorities are generally to achieve independence, to have a place of your own and to possess a long list of consumer products such as cars. If you have children when you are on a low income this will add extra responsibilities to your own 'developmental' needs.

It may be a matter of opinion, but it seems to me that it is no bad thing to be a little financially irresponsible at this stage. Risk-taking, speculative investment in a business and general experimentation in life are important ways of gaining experience and finding out just what your own capacities really are.

If your circumstances allow it, the most sensible investment to make is probably to get a toe-hold on the housing ladder. This will usually entail taking out a mortgage, which is the cheapest form of borrowing available to the public, but your repayments should approximate to the cost of renting. It is essential not to borrow too much since you may lose your property if you fail to keep up the repayments; the main mortgage lenders do their best to ensure that your borrowing requirements are realistic. Property is discussed in more detail in Chapter 10, but here the main point to be aware of is that financing your own home through a mortgage is actually an effective way of saving – by repaying a mortgage over a number of years you are accumulating a capital sum in the form of the 'equity' in your home.

Stage 2 The future-building years – the thirties

By the time you are in your thirties certain realities begin to emerge. You may have entered into a long-term romantic relationship and have produced children. The chances are that you have made some progress in your career and are earning more than ever before. This brings us to three social phenomena that can have a profound effect on your finances.

- Divorce
- Losing your job
- Bringing up children

These are so important that they are dealt with separately on pages 23 and 24; the characteristic that they have in common is that they are all extremely costly.

Stage 2 is the time for planning for the future. If you are able to do so, you should set about acquiring a property if you have not done so already – this will normally entail saving money for several years in order to accumulate a deposit. You may be a member of a pension scheme, and if you are not it is advisable to consider joining one or contributing to a PEP (see Chapter 6). With some 30 years to go before the state retirement age, a programme of regular saving towards a pension has plenty of time in which to accumulate into a sizable sum through compounding and investment growth.

Education and child care are expensive, even if you choose to rely on the state for most of the cost. The older children get, the more expensive they become, so some kind of medium-term savings plan is helpful – say for a period of ten years or so.

It is at stage 2 that the foundations for acquiring wealth are laid. If you are able to save some of what you earn over many years you will accumulate capital. It is the dull, steady method for achieving affluence which is sometimes called 'deferred gratification' – you forego some pleasures now in order to have more of them in the future.

Stage 3 Middle age – the forties and fifties

Middle ages is generally the time when your earning power is at its peak. If you reach the top of your profession your income may continue to increase for decades, but you will be in a minority if this occurs.

Stage 3 people have the life experience to be able to manage their investments actively if they wish. If you have accumulated some capital by this time, you still have at least ten years in which to make it grow. As we saw in Chapter 1, the return you will achieve will largely depend upon the degree of risk that you are prepared to take. Stage 3 is the time when people are more likely to invest directly in the stock market with a view to obtaining substantial growth. Some people stay out of shares altogether, however, and concentrate on more 'understandable' investments such as property, while others leave their employers to start businesses. Business start ups are examined in Chapter 12, where it is argued that many people who start businesses do not appreciate just how high the risks really are, particularly if you borrow heavily. While it may be true that entrepreneurs can be made as well as born, actively running a business is as skilled a profession as medicine or the law, so if you are entrepreneur material it may be better to start earlier in life.

If you have developed some investment skills, Stage 3 is paradoxically a good time for taking stock market risks, but before you do so it would be wise already to have:

● your own home
● a pension and/or a PEP scheme
● life insurance if you have dependents
● cash savings against emergencies

The reason for this is that you need diversification and security to protect yourself against possible losses.

Stage 4 Retirement – the sixties and beyond

Ideally, Stage 4 is a time for enjoying life and benefiting from all that deferred gratification you have practised in previous years. Some people continue to work and earn high incomes, but most will want to be drawing an income from their accumulated savings and pension funds.

No-one really knows how long they will live, and it is unwise to make any precise assumptions. If, for example, you decide that you will die before the age of 80 and spend all your savings accordingly, you may suffer if you live longer than this. Most Stage 4 people are looking for an income and inflation protection from their savings, rather than substantial capital growth. A great deal depends on how much capital you have accumulated in the previous years – and by this time many people will have inherited lump sums from relatives which will supplement their savings. In general, borrowings are reduced to the minimum, mortgages are paid off and investments are in property, bonds and the 'safer' shares.

Stage 4 people tend to be risk-averse – they are more concerned about protecting what they have rather than trying to acquire more. There are good reasons for this, since health-care costs may increase dramatically, and changes to the tax and welfare systems can easily pauperise elderly people. As you get older, administrative chores become increasingly burdensome, so safety becomes more important than squeezing the last penny out of every transaction – this is when good long-term relationships with trusted advisers really pay off, in terms of the peace of mind they give you.

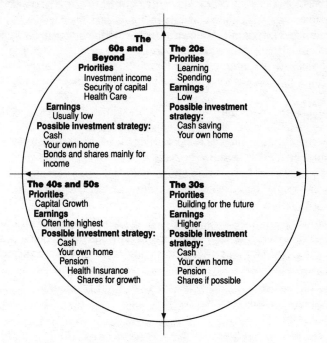

Figure 2.1 The four financial stages in adulthood

The deferment of gratification

The investment strategy described above is quintessentially middle class. It is a traditional method for attaining affluence at low risk, and has the advantage that it can cope with many of the financial problems that arise during life. It is not the only way of becoming rich, however, nor is it absolutely risk-free. As has already been discussed, becoming very rich essentially means being willing to take greater risks, and having the physical and emotional stamina to bounce back from defeat. Perhaps more surprising is the fact that the deferred gratification strategy is not risk free; to understand why this is, you have to consider the past. Theorists tell us that large parts of the middle classes are wiped out financially every 60 years or so due to political events beyond their control. Here are a few examples:

- During the hyper-inflation in Germany after World War I many respectable German widows literally starved to death because their savings, which were mainly in bonds, lost their value.
- The upper classes in Britain saw their wealth evaporate between 1890 and 1920 due to dramatic political and economic changes.
- The wealthy planters in the southern states of the US were stripped of their assets after the American Civil War in the last century.
- Anglo-Irish landowners lost their estates during the period leading up to the creation of the Irish Republic in World War I.
- The recent bankrupting of many private 'names' in the Lloyds insurance market is arguably related to political changes in the US, where courts are making huge awards against companies in asbestosis and pollution cases, with the insurers having to bear the massive costs.

Despite what the politicians tell us, there really is no reason to believe that the future will be more perfect than the past – so asset-owners may be unfortunate enough to suffer substantial losses through no fault of their own. As ever, the best defence against this is diversification into different asset classes, including putting some money abroad (see Chapter 9).

The medium-term effects of divorce, job loss and children

These three life events are costly, unpredictable and can put tremendous strains on your financial commitments. The purpose of examining them here is simply to see their effect on your finances – no moral judgements are intended.

Divorce

Divorce is more expensive than most people imagine, due principally to the high cost of lawyers' fees. The longer it takes to come to a settlement, the higher these fees will be. No doubt many solicitors would like to see a reform of the system, but as it stands, it is they who benefit financially, not the spouses!

- Even if you are the spouse who is a net receiver of money, you are still a loser. Where once the costs of living were shared, there now must be two households. Even if your ex-spouse is supporting you and the children, you are not assured that this money will continue to be paid, since he or she may simply lose hope of ever getting free of this cost, and simply give up working.
- For both spouses, regular financial commitments such as mortgage repayments, pension contributions and life insurance premiums are often disrupted by the divorce, so if you have not made sure that the contracts allow you to suspend payments for a period you may suffer quite heavy penalties.
- When the assets are divided, it often happens that they are sold for less than their market value. In this sense, divorce is similar to the liquidation of a company – the owners of the assets actually receive substantially less than their true value. This is because people often lose their heads, and are so keen to put an end to the proceedings that they are willing to take the loss. Cash generally becomes very important, especially where one of the spouses has not been working for some years, so assets, usually houses, are liquidated to provide funds which are spent on living expenses.

The effect of all these costs and losses is to reduce the size of your accumulated capital in a much shorter time than it took to acquire it. Friendly, unhurried divorces between two people who are fair-minded are the cheapest kind.

Losing your job

We are going through an era of drastic re-organisation of business, and many people can expect to change their careers and retrain more than once during their working lives. The main effects of losing your job are:

- a sudden drop in income
- inability to make payments to pension schemes, insurances and, possibly, borrowings

There are various types of insurance available to protect against this hiccup to some degree, but they tend to be expensive. The really important thing to do if you lose your job is to reduce your borrowings to a manageable level until you get a new job. This takes an adaptability and strength of mind that is difficult to develop, especially if you have not gone through the experience before.

As mentioned earlier, it is vital that you check that there are no penalties for suspending payments into pension schemes and the rest **before** you sign up. This means that it is important to plan for the possibility of losing your job when there isn't a cloud on the horizon.

Bringing up children

For the last few decades the state has played a dominant role in the raising of children, and a by-product of this is that many parents have become psychologically dependent on the state system. This would not be a problem, perhaps, if it weren't for the global trend towards the dismantling of state social welfare – someone who has a new baby today cannot possibly know what the state benefit and education systems will provide 10 or 15 years from now. For this reason, it is prudent to set aside sums in a fund which you specifically earmark for your children's benefit, whether it is to be used for private education, or simply for holidays, clothes and extra-curricular activities. Clearly, the amount you spend on your children largely depends on your income, but even if you are on a low income it makes sense to save for this purpose. If you are a tax-payer, it would make sense to use a PEP scheme for the purpose (see Chapter 6).

Investing in the medium and long-term

Short-term investing refers to periods of under five years, medium-term to periods of between 5 and 15 years, and long-term to periods over 15 years. By setting your objectives in the context of your life stage, it is a relatively simple matter to assign the length of time you need for any particular investment plan designed to meet a particular objective.

EXAMPLE

Mary and John are married and aged 30, so they are Stage 2 people. They both work, and are planning to purchase their first house and raise a family. They decide that their main objectives are:

- to own their own home
- to join a pension scheme
- to save money for their children
- to save a fund in cash for emergencies

Purchasing a house by way of a mortgage is a long-term commitment – normally a mortgage lasts for 25 years. If they buy well and the market moves in their favour, they may be able to pay off their mortgage early, but they need to ensure that they can easily handle the repayments out of their monthly income.

John is a civil servant, so he is eligible for a generous 'final salary scheme' pension, which is a long-term commitment. He discusses his options with an independent adviser, and decides to increase his contributions slightly.

Mary's employer does not offer a pension scheme, so if she wants to save for retirement the options are either to take out a personal pension plan (which is less cost-effective than an occupational scheme) or to save in some other way, such as in a PEP scheme.

Saving money for children is a medium-term objective. John and Mary decide to use John's annual PEP entitlement of up to £6,000 in a General PEP to save money for their children.

Saving cash is a short-term objective. Since John and Mary are both tax-payers, they decide to save what cash they can in TESSAs (see Chapter 4), which allows them to save a maximum of £9,000 each in a tax-advantageous way. TESSA schemes are fairly flexible, so they know that if they need the money before the end of the TESSA scheme they can withdraw it, although there will be a penalty.

After all this there isn't much money left for household expenses and holidays – a typical Stage 2 situation! John and Mary accept that they must forego some pleasures now in order to reach their future objectives.

Reviewing your current circumstances

Not everyone wants to have, or can get, a secure, structured job, but this does not mean that they cannot save and invest! If your future is uncertain, it simply means that certain types of financial commitment are less attractive. Self-employed people on irregular incomes, for example, may find it difficult to raise a mortgage unless they have a large percentage of the purchase price of a home already. The answer is to save regularly through one of the methods outlined in this book until you have accumulated enough capital to spread your wings a little wider. Those of us who wish to follow risky careers, such as acting or music, may have to forego most conventional financial plans for many years, but even so, it is advisable to save a proportion of your income.

It is a good idea to review your financial commitments and plans at least once a year. Not only will your own circumstances change from time to time, but there will also be changes in the economy and taxation system which will make different types of investment more or less attractive in relation to one another. In the next chapter we will look at the various types of financial adviser available; once you have found an adviser with whom you are comfortable, it would be helpful to conduct your review with your adviser's help, since he or she may know of developments which could affect your plans.

Calculating your net worth

Your net worth is the 'score' in the game of investment. Most people do not have an accurate idea of their net worth – in fact, very rich people find it almost impossible to value all their assets accurately – but a regular check on your net worth will give you a good indication of how well your investment projects are going.

Step 1

First of all, write down the values of each of your assets. A list of your assets may include the following.

● Your home – write down the realistic sale value, net of professional fees, minus the amount of mortgage outstanding. If you have an endowment mortgage, there is an added complication in that the value of the endowment may not, in some cases, exactly match the outstanding mortgage; check the growth of the endowment policy with your lender.
● Your car – the realistic value you would get if you sold it quickly.
● Valuables – jewellery and other valuables at their insurance valuation (but remember, if you ever have to sell them in a hurry you will probably get less than 50% of this valuation).
● White goods – these are appliances such as washing machines and freezers. Write down what you think you would realistically get for them if you advertised them locally (this will be much less than their new price).
● Pension – the current value of any fund you have.
● Life assurance – the surrender value of any policies.
● Savings – these may include Building Society deposits, bank deposits, and National Savings certificates.
● Investments – the market values of shares, unit trusts (bid price), bonds and other investments.

Add up the total.

Step 2

Now make a list of your liabilities. We cheated a little by deducting the mortgage from the value of your home already, but this was because the loan is secured on the house. If you have an endowment mortgage, put down the estimated sale value of your house and the estimated value of your policy on the assets list, and the corresponding loan on the liabilities list.

Write down all your other debts, and the rates of interest that apply (you will find the interest rates in the paperwork).

- Credit cards – each type of card, the current total due as of the last statement plus any purchases you have made since then.
- Shop debt – what you owe on storecards and accounts.
- Bank loans – outstanding amounts, plus the monthly payment and the number of months to the end of the term.
- Bank overdraft – the amount currently outstanding.
- Hire purchase agreements – the monthly payments and the number of months to the end of the term.
- Finance company loans – the payments and the period left until the end of the term.
- Informal loans – for example, from friends and relatives.

Add up the total.

Step 3

Subtract the Step 2 total from the Step 1 total; the result is your 'net worth'. Now that you know your net worth, you have a benchmark by which to measure your progress in the future. The lists and calculations you have made are your 'balance sheet'; date it and file it for future reference.

EXAMPLE

Joan is 45, divorced and with grown-up children. Her net worth is £200,000, of which £50,000 is available for growth investments. Currently this money is in a unit trust. Joan is considering putting this money into other investments, and has interviewed a stockbroker with a view to investing directly in equities. After a great deal of thought, she decides to go ahead with this plan. Her broker understands that she is prepared to hold equities for the medium to long term and is seeking to obtain growth rather than income, so all dividends and other payments will be reinvested.

After a year, Joan reviews her net worth again. Most of her money is in her own home, and she reckons that she would

---

get about 5% less if she sold her house, a loss of £5,000. Her stock market portfolio, however, has grown by 10%, giving her a paper profit of £5,000. Her other investments have also grown in value, largely because she is making contributions to them out of her income, and she finds that her net worth is around £210,000, which represents 5% annual growth. She then makes an adjustment for inflation, using the RPI, which has been, say 3%, over the past year, so a rough and ready inflation adjustment means that her net worth in terms of last year's money value is:

	210,000
less 3%	6,300
Total	203,700

Thus, her net worth has grown by less than 4% in real terms. Joan is not concerned, however, because she takes the view that her holdings are for the long term, and that over time her investments will show a better annual rate of growth than this.

—— Investment and personality ——

It is a common-place in the financial markets to say that investment is affected by two main emotions, fear and greed. This may sound ugly, but it is perfectly true. During economic downturns and market collapses, the majority of people are affected by fear, and liquidate their assets at knock-down prices, During booms, the majority become greedy and pour more and more of their money into investments, certain that they can only go up. In both cases, the effect is that a particular investment class becomes over- or under-valued, which creates opportunity for those wily individuals who have the foresight to move against the trend.

EXAMPLE

During the mid-1980s, the UK saw a dramatic boom in house prices. As is usually the case, the people most terrified by this phenomenon were the least experienced, namely the people who had not purchased a home before. To them, it seemed as if house prices were going to continue to output inflation forever, and if they didn't buy a property as soon as possible, they would never be able to do so. The high prices and loose borrowing controls meant that many people borrowed large sums. Then, in 1989, interest rates started to rise, which increased repayment costs, and prices started to fall. In fact, the housing market collapsed, causing a dramatic rise in the number of repossessions and creating the hitherto relatively unknown phenomenon of 'negative equity', where some owners' debts were higher than the market value of their properties. The press fuelled the public's anguish, and some incautious pundits were heard to say that property would never again be a good investment. At the time of writing (summer 1996), we have had several years of low inflation and interest rates, and it looks as if prices are stabilising and that we may be in for a period of increasing house prices once again. Those property owners who have been able to ride out the bad times, and who have bought good-value homes, may well be rewarded with a good return within the next few years.

Going against the general mood is just about the most difficult action you can take in investment, and can be the most rewarding. It takes a lot of courage, knowledge and good judgement – qualities which not everyone possesses. For this reason, responsible advisers usually err on the side of caution when counselling their clients to minimise the possible short-term effects of dramatic falls in the markets.

Here is a short questionnaire to help you think about your personal attitudes towards risk.

1 You have a trusted friend who is an expert computer programmer and business person. He is looking for backers for a scheme to produce a ground-breaking computer program which could produce very high returns, up to 80 times the initial investment, if it is successful. If it fails, you will lose your money. Your friend estimates that the chances of success are 1 in 5 within four years, based on a business plan which has been independently checked. How much would you invest?

A   Nothing   C   A quarter's wages
B   A month's wages   D   Half a year's wages

2 You inherit your grandmother's house, which is in a bad state of
   repair and is worth about £80,000. If you let it out as it is, you
   could get £360 a month for it. If you borrowed £6,000 pounds and
   were prepared to do some of the renovation yourself, you could get
   about £800 a month for it after a few month's work. Would you:
   A   Sell the property now?
   B   Rent it out in its present state?
   C   Renovate the house and let it, with a view to selling some
       time in the future?

3 You are a participant in a game show on television and are offered
   several choices. Which one would you take?
   A   £500 now
   B   A 1 in 2 chance of winning 2,000 pounds
   C   A 1 in 5 chance of winning 5,000 pounds
   D   A 1 in 20 chance of winning 50,000 pounds

4 You buy some shares, and three weeks later you find that their
   price has dropped by 12%. You have studied the company's
   circumstances thoroughly, and you can't see any fundamental reason for thinking that the company is any less valuable than it was
   three weeks ago. Your broker can't explain why the price has
   dropped. Would you:
   A   Buy more shares because they are even better value than they
       were?
   B   Sell the shares and accept the loss?
   C   Do nothing, and wait for the price to rise again?

Now add up your score:

1 A – 1, B – 3, C – 6, D – 9
2 A – 1, B – 2, C – 3
3 A – 1, B – 3, C – 5, D – 9
4 A – 4, B – 1, C – 3

If you scored 9 or less, you are probably a cautious person. Stay with
low-risk investments which give low returns. If you scored between 10
and 16 you probably don't mind taking medium-level risks in the
search for above-average returns. If you scored more than 16 you
probably enjoy the thrills and spills of high-risk taking with the
chance of making exceptional gains.

All this may be 'pop' psychology, but there is a serious point to it, which is that you must get to know how much risk you are generally willing to take. Everyone is different, and with experience your attitudes may change – some people can sleep soundly at night with massive debts hanging over their heads, while others become desperate at the prospect of a minor loss. By getting to know your own feelings about risk you can develop a strategy to suit yourself.

3
GETTING GOOD FINANCIAL ADVICE

In this chapter we will look at:

- The Financial Services Act
- The problem of fraud
- The Securities and Investments Board (SIB)
- The range of financial advisers
- Questions to ask your advisers

The Financial Services Act

The formal regulation of the financial markets is a relatively new development which came in with the Financial Services Act 1986. The Act created wide-ranging statutory powers and a number of new criminal offences, all with the laudable aim of protecting individuals, whether they are investors, borrowers, or simply members of pension or insurance schemes. If the UK is to have strong financial markets which can compete internationally, so the thinking goes, it is essential that both professionals and the public have confidence that they are properly regulated.

Here are the main features of the regulatory regime

- Advertising must give warnings about the volatility and marketability of the financial products on offer.
- Investment businesses must be authorised by a regulatory body.

- Investors have a right to be given details of charges, fees, commissions and any other payments earned by their advisers and agents selling financial products.
- Investment businesses must keep their clients' money separate from their own.
- Investment businesses must act fairly towards their clients, know their general circumstances and give their 'best advice'.
- The Investor's Compensation Scheme will make payments of up to £48,000 per private investor if an authorised investment business goes bust. Some professionals, such as solicitors, are excluded from the scheme, but are covered by other compensation schemes.
- Except for life insurance and unit trusts, investment businesses cannot make unsolicited telephone calls and visits to customers.
- Investment businesses must follow a specified procedure for dealing with complaints, and customers can complain to the relevant regulatory body if they are not satisfied.
- Published investment advice, such as is given in newsletters and 'tip sheets', must be authorised and cannot contain misleading information. Newspapers are exempt from this rule.

The problem of fraud

Any process involving large sums of money is tempting to fraudsters, so investors need to keep on their toes.

The Financial Services Act gives a good deal of protection, but no system can be 100% effective. As a private investor, you must bear some of the responsibility for guarding against fraud, at the very least by acting cautiously, especially if you are being invited to invest in a scheme that promises unusually high returns.

Keep in mind that if you are a victim of fraud:

- you may have to wait for a long time before recovering your money even if you are covered by the Investor's Compensation Scheme, and that
- high legal costs can make it impossible for an individual to pursue a determined fraudster through the courts

Ponzi schemes

The classic large-scale fraud is known as the 'Ponzi scheme', named after a notorious pre-war fraud in the USA. A Ponzi scheme may appear to be a highly respectable concern dealing in sound investments. To work, it has to be popular and growing – the first investors receive their returns from money paid into the scheme by later investors.

Normally, only a part of the funds coming into the scheme are ever legitimately invested. Ponzi schemes work so long as there are new investors coming forward with enough money to keep the prior investors happy. Eventually the money dries up and the scheme collapses. It is a characteristic of Ponzi schemes that their promoters do not believe that they have done anything wrong, and persist in declaring their innocence even after serving a prison sentence.

Ponzi schemes are difficult to detect in the early stages because they have the appearance of legitimate schemes. The Barlow Clowes scandal, where private investors believed that they were putting their money into gilts (see Chapter 4) at advantageous rates through a loophole known as 'bond washing', was not discovered until some years after it began.

EXAMPLE

Kevin says he runs a factoring business which buys due invoices from small companies at a discount, making a profit when the invoice is settled by the customer. He is seeking short-term loans to finance the operation, and promises to pay the money back with 25% interest within nine months.

All the money that Kevin raises is used to support his extravagant lifestyle. When the first loans become due he persuades most of the investors to keep their money in the scheme and pays off the few people who want to pull out using money raised from new investors. When the scheme finally collapses Kevin is nowhere to be found.

Pyramid schemes

These are usually more obvious than Ponzi schemes but people still fall for them. Essentially they work on the principle of a 'chain letter'.

EXAMPLE

Kevin invites Alice, Bob and four others to buy the right to distribute a product for £5,000 each. As distributors, they can sell the product and, in addition, sell distributorships to other people, splitting the money 50/50 with Kevin. Kevin points out that you only have to find two new distributors to recoup your investment, and that they should be able to sign up six new people every three months.

Sound interesting? Look what happens if Kevin sells six distributorships, and each distributor signs up six more people each quarter:

Quarter	Number of distributors	Quarter	Number of distributors
1	6	7	279,936
2	36	8	1,679,616
3	216	9	10,044,696
4	1,296	10	60,466,176
5	7,776	11	362,797,056
6	46,656	12	2,176,782,336
		13	13,060,694,016

Thus, on Kevin's figures, in the fourth year more than the entire population of the world will have become distributors! If you point this out to him he may take you aside and tell you not to worry – by the time that happens, you will have got your money back. The trouble is that you will rarely be able to establish how far up the pyramid you stand; there may be thousands of other Kevins running around signing up distributors already.

Avoiding fraud

Anyone can be tricked sometimes, so no-one can be certain that they will never be the victims of fraud. Solicitors, for example, are notoriously easy 'marks' for certain types of swindle. Frauds often depend on short time scales, so take your time to think things over before investing in anything. Here are some other tactics you can use.

- Avoid 'once in a lifetime' opportunities, or what are sometimes called 'red ribbon' deals because they are so convincingly presented – all you have to do is invest and the growth rate will be astonishing, you are told. The only deals worth having are the ones you create yourself in a business, and they always involve hard work.
- Visit the premises of the business and look around. Try to get an impression of the substance and intelligence of the staff.
- 'Comparison shop' ruthlessly – as a passive investor, it is unlikely that you will be offered anything truly unique, so take the trouble to interview several firms which offer comparable services.
- Make a thorough check on the firm. If it is a limited company, for example, you can obtain its published accounts from Companies House (see Useful Addresses). Most professionals will be listed in directories which you can find in large public libraries. Ask around to see if anyone you know knows them, and what their experiences have been.
- Telephone the Securities and Investment Board (SIB) to check that the adviser is registered, and ascertain exactly what he or she is authorised to do.
- Avoid the trap of thinking, 'these people are making such confident claims that they must be telling the truth. No-one would be stupid enough to lie – it wouldn't be worth it' Fraudsters' motives can be very obscure and they often do not behave rationally.

The Securities and Investments Board (SIB)

The SIB is a private limited company, not a government department, with legal powers to implement the Financial Services Act. It is an 'umbrella organisation', and oversees a number of other regulatory bodies which are divided into two types.

- Self-regulating organisations (SROs)
- Recognised professional bodies (RPBs).

You should only ever go for professional financial advice to someone who is a member of an SRO or an RPB – this is your first line of defence should anything go wrong.

Self-regulating organisations (SROs)

As their name suggests, SROs are 'self-regulating' – in other words, the SROs are managed by individuals from the relevant industry. It has been suggested that this does not make SROs as independent as the public would like. The SROs are as follows.

- SFA (the Securities and Futures Authority) which regulates the operators in the future and equities markets, including stock brokers.
- IMRO (the Investment Management Regulatory Organisation), which regulates fund managers, including those of unit trusts and pension funds.
- PIA (Personal Investment Authority), which has taken over the FIMBRA (the Financial Intermediaries, Managers and Brokers Regulatory Organisation) and LAUTRO (the Life Assurance and Unit Trust Regulatory Organisation). The PIA essentially oversees the heavily packaged financial products aimed at consumers, such as life assurance and unit trusts.

Some organisations are members of more than one SRO.

Recognised professional bodies (RPBs)

Most professional bodies on the periphery of finance are regulated by one of the nine recognised professional bodies (RPBs) which are also answerable to the SIB. They are:

- The Law Society of England and Wales
- The Law Society of Northern Ireland
- The Law Society of Scotland
- The Institute of Chartered Accountants in England and Wales
- The Institute of Chartered Accountants in Scotland
- The Institute of Chartered Accountants in Ireland
- The Chartered Association of Certified Accountants
- The Insurance Brokers Registration Council
- The Institute of Actuaries

— The range of financial advisers —

The range is very wide, partly because no single adviser can be an expert in all financial matters, and partly because there is a good deal of money to be made out of giving advice. The fact that an adviser makes money should not deter you – if the advice is really good, it will be worth the cost. Not every adviser is really good, though; some are little more than inexperienced salesmen with not much training.

Since there are so many specialist advisers, it is a good idea to develop an ongoing relationship with several different ones. This way, you can build up a better picture of the overall approach to take, and benefit from their different areas of expertise.

Here are some of the main advisers you are likely to encounter.

	Tied or Independent	Area of expertise	Possible fault
Independent financial advisers	Independent	Depends on background	Lack of experience
Accountants	Independent	Taxation General business	Narrow view
Solicitors	Independent	A special area of the law	Slow and cautious
Bank managers	Tied	Borrowing	Pushing the wrong products
Building society managers	Tied	Mortgages	Pushing the wrong products
Insurance company representatives	Tied	Own company's product	Lack of experience/ supervision
Insurance brokers	Independent	General insurance market Making claims	May favour certain companies
Stockbrokers	Regulated by SIB	Stocks and shares Investment generally	May encourage too much buying and selling of investments

Figure 3.1 Picking an adviser

Tied agents

Tied agents represent a company, most often an insurance company, and only sell the products offered by that company. They don't have to tell you how much commission they are making, but they do have to tell you that they are tied. High street banks and most building societies are tied agents. Tied agents are backed by large companies, so they are unlikely to go bust, and they may, sometimes, be able to give you the best deal on a particular product. Never sign an agreement that includes a penalty clause where you have to pay a tied agent a sum of money if you allow an insurance policy or a mortgage to lapse. Note that tied agents are not directly regulated under the Financial Services Act; their companies are responsible for the wrongdoing of tied agents, but it is not clear how far this liability extends.

Independent financial advisers (IFAs)

These are people who may or may not have an impressive set of qualifications; the only professional qualification that they must have is the Financial Planning Certificate. IFAs have to tell you all about their charges and commissions, and must give you the best independent advice they can. IFAs may either charge you a fee for their advice, or take a commission from the company from which you purchase a product. If you pay a fee, ask the adviser to rebate any commissions to you.

Accountants

Not all accountants will give advice, but those that do are IFAs. Their great area of expertise is usually taxation, but check their qualifications and experience closely. Experienced accountants may know a great deal about business in general.

Solicitors

These will also be IFAs. Their area of expertise will be in certain aspects of the law, and you should try to find out which aspects these are. As a rule they are a cautious breed and don't necessarily know much about business. They have a tendency to charge highly for their time, and they tend to take a lot of time.

Bank managers

Gone are the days of the wise old bank manager who knew all his customers intimately. Nowadays, you are more likely to find that your 'personal account manager' changes every year or two. They are tied agents and under pressure to sell you a host of financial products. Their area of expertise is in lending and cash flow; if you are thinking of borrowing, it is worth hearing what they have to say, even if you go somewhere else to borrow.

Building society managers

Most of these are tied. Their area of expertise is mortgages. Building societies are becoming more like banks every day.

Insurance company representatives

These are tied. They should know their own products backwards and be able to explain what is a complicated subject clearly. Don't sign up for anything without getting opinions from other kinds of adviser first.

Insurance brokers

These may be tied or independent. The good ones know a great deal about the ins and outs of different insurance companies, and, even more importantly, how to make sure that the companies actually pay out if you claim, which depends a great deal on the wording of the policy and the information that you give when you take the policy out.

Stock brokers

A bona fide stock broker must be a member of the SFA. A good broker could be the best adviser you ever have, but the increased corporatisation of the industry has raised questions about the impartiality of some brokers working for large companies. Brokers offer a range of services for dealing in investments, and their charges vary widely. Remember that brokers are remunerated in the main by commissions on transactions, rather than on the success of an investment, so the more you buy and sell the more money they make.

— Questions to ask your advisers —

These may seem extremely cheeky questions, but it is your money, and you have every right to ask them. Try to get the answers to all of these in writing.

1 Are you an independent adviser or are you tied?
2 Which regulatory body are you authorised by? Are you fully authorised?
3 Will you refer me to satisfied customers whom I can ask about the quality of your services?
4 Do you have professional indemnity insurance? With what company? (This insurance will pay out claims if you have to sue the adviser for some reason.)
5 How long have you worked in the advice industry and what companies have you worked for in the last ten years?
6 What is your conduct record with your regulatory body? Have you ever been interviewed by them on disciplinary matters?
7 Are you an agent for any financial service company, and if so, who?
8 What will be your commission, if any, on the transactions you advise?
9 What are your charges in detail?
10 What is the risk to my money?
11 Why are you advising me to do these things?
12 Are you authorised to handle my cash, or do my cheques have to be made out to the company which I buy the financial product from? (The latter is probably safer even if the adviser is authorised to handle cash.)

Here are some additional questions to ask stockbrokers; in each case, the answer should be 'yes'.

13 Do you subscribe to the Reuters and Extel information services?
14 Will you provide information from these services for free?
15 Do you execute orders immediately on receipt of my instructions?

Conclusion

In an ideal world you would develop intimate long-term relationships with two or three advisers in different fields, and conduct regular reviews with them – say, every year or two, and whenever your circumstances changed significantly. If you are fortunate enough to find advisers with whom you can do this, you will have a battery of experience and financial wisdom on your side. Getting such relationships takes effort, good judgement and time – they are like marriages, and shouldn't usually be rushed. In the meantime, take things slowly and don't sign up for long-term commitments without taking the trouble to:

- think them over carefully
- read up on them in the financial press
- discuss them with more experienced friends and relatives
- make sure you understand your choices

Remember, the more effort you put in to understanding your finances, the more your advisers will be able to help you – ultimately, you are your own best adviser!

4
CASH AND BONDS

This kind of investment is essentially money-lending to industry and government. We look at:

- Cash
  - Risk
  - Choosing where to save
  - Tax on interest
  - TESSAs
  - National Savings products
- Bonds

Cash

Despite the problem of inflation there are still very good reasons to save cash.

We all need cash for emergencies, and it is better to use cash savings, which have earned interest, than to borrow cash at high interest rates.

While some argue that you should keep your cash savings as low as possible, others suggest keeping, say, the equivalent of three or six month's net salary in cash, while others argue it is better to keep a percentage of your net worth – say between 5% and 10% – in cash at all times, but usually they include bonds within their definition of cash. It largely depends on your individual circumstances and on what kind of person you are, so, within the limits outlined above, it makes sense to keep that sum in cash which makes you feel 'comfortable'.

Cash savings lose their value over the long term during periods of inflation, so you really keep it for its liquidity, not for its potential for growth. Nevertheless, it is worth getting some interest on the deposits, since you may achieve some growth in the short term, or at least mitigate the effects of inflation.

Risk

When depositing money, you should always consider the risk that the deposit-taker will not pay you back. Here are a few points.

- UK bank deposits of up to £20,000 are protected by a deposit protection fund which will pay you 75% of the value of the deposit if the bank goes bust. This means that if you want to have more than £20,000 deposited in a bank, you should split it up amongst different banks to keep the protection. Check that your bank is covered by the scheme – BCCI, the international bank which went spectacularly bust, wasn't.
- Building society deposits are protected to 90% of the first £20,000, so they offer better protection than bank deposits.

This level of protection is very good by international standards, so in general there is little to worry about, as long as the organisation you are using is covered.

Choosing where to save

Your choice depends upon two essential factors:

- how long can you tie your money up for?
- how quickly can you get your money out if you need it in a hurry, and are there penalties for early withdrawal?

In general, the longer you are willing to tie up your money for, and the less priority you place on early, and instant, withdrawals, the better the rates will be. Once you have decided on these points, you can then compare providers in terms of:

- the interest rates they offer for the size of the deposit you are making,

- the penalties for withdrawals and
- the charge, if any, for transferring the funds to another scheme

It is sometimes helpful to compare the net rate offered with the tax-free rate obtainable from National Savings products.

There is a large range of cash deposit packages available, and they can be very confusing, all claiming great benefits for their particular combination of interest rate, 'lock-in' period and tax advantages, if any. Most of them only exist because there is intense competition for your money amongst the financial services businesses, and the advertising tends to play on people's fears.

If you are investing in other ways as well, the interest rate you are getting on your emergency cash fund is not worth worrying about too much. It is certainly not worth spending hours each week debating whether or not to move it to another account offering a fraction of a percentage more – use the time to look for more rewarding investment opportunities!

In general, banks change their interest rates more frequently than building societies do. Unless you are a keen follower of interest rates and the economy, choosing the right deposit account can be a chore – most of us aren't very good at knowing how long we can tie up our cash savings for, and penalties for early withdrawals can cancel out any benefits you might have got from a slightly higher interest rate. One practical approach is as follows.

- Have a current account or a combined current/deposit account.
- Save up to a few thousand (say £5,000) in a deposit account of some kind as emergency money. The difference in interest rates won't make all that much difference to what is a relatively small sum.
- Don't worry too much about relative interest rates, but check charges and penalties carefully before committing yourself.

Tax on interest

In most types of account, the interest you earn is taxed. If you are a higher rate taxpayer you will have to pay the difference between the tax which is deducted automatically from the interest and the higher rate when you pay your income taxes. Banks and building societies usually quote two rates of interest, the 'gross' rate and the 'net' rate.

The gross rate is the amount before tax, and the net rate is the amount after the tax has been deducted.

Some of the deposit types offer some or all the interest tax free, while others pay interest gross. Non-taxpayers can reclaim tax deducted from bank and building society accounts by completing an Inland Revenue claim form either when they open the account or at the point when they become non-taxpayers.

TESSAs

Banks, building societies and incorporated friendly societies can offer tax-exempt special savings accounts, known as TESSAs. These were launched in 1991 for everyone over 18. Married couples can each have a separate TESSA. If you keep to the rules, the interest on the account is free of tax, but if you break the rules, the interest will suffer tax at the investor's highest rate for the fiscal year in which the breach of the rules occurs.

When TESSAs first became available, they had enormous appeal because most interest rates offered a real return above inflation, and TESSAs offered an exceptional return. By late 1993, the fall in interest rates generally meant that even TESSAs were being closed in order for capital to be moved into risk investments with potential for higher growth.

TESSA rules

The main rule is that the capital deposited must not be withdrawn for five years. The net interest can be withdrawn without penalty during the five year period.

If you withdraw more than the net interest, the account loses its tax-free status. Thus, if the basic rate of tax is 25%, a TESSA holder cannot withdraw more than 75% of the interest from the account without breaking the rule.

The maximum amount that can be invested in a TESSA over five years is £9,000. Up to £150 can be invested on a regular monthly basis, or deposits can be of irregular amounts to suit the saver's convenience. However, not more than £3,000 may be invested in the first year and not more than £1,800 in each of the other four years. An investor who deposits less than the maximum amount in any one year cannot make up that amount by exceeding the maximum in future years. Most providers set a minimum deposit, but this can be as low as £1.

TESSAs usually pay much more attractive interest rates than normal bank and building society rates for the same amount of capital. However, the interest rate is variable. After five years, the TESSA matures and loses its tax-free status. The investor can either withdraw the total investment tax free, or leave the money in the account, where whatever interest the provider pays thereafter will be liable to income tax at the investor's highest tax rate.

When the TESSA matures

When the TESSA matures, the investor is allowed to replace it by a new TESSA with its own five-year term. Originally, the rules for the second TESSA were identical to those for the first. For example, the maximum deposit in the first year would be £3,000 and the total invested over the whole of the second five-year period £9,000.

However, the danger of large capital outflows from building societies when the first TESSAs matured in 1996 was such that these rules were changed in the November 1994 budget. As the TESSAs mature, investors will be allowed to transfer all the capital they invested in their first TESSA into a new one, but they will not be allowed to transfer the interest earned on the first TESSA into the second. Thus, people who invested the maximum amount in their first TESSA will be able to open a new TESSA with £9,000 instead of £3,000. However, they will not be able to deposit additional amounts into their TESSA over the next five years.

People who invested less than £9,000 in their original TESSA will be able to add to their initial deposit over the next five years until the maximum allowed for each stage under the rules is reached. None of the foregoing applies to people who are investing in TESSAs for the first time.

Transferring a TESSA

Deposits can be transferred from one provider's TESSA to another with higher interest rates. Some providers charge a penalty for transfer, examples of which include a flat fee of £25, a loss of one month's interest or a loss of 90 days' interest. Such penalties are often associated with above-average TESSA interest rates.

'Feeder' accounts

Many providers will open separate accounts for up to £9,000 maximum investment. This account will earn interest at normal (taxed) rates, and 'drip feed' money into the TESSA on the due dates for each annual instalment. Transfer of a TESSA is much more likely to attract a penalty when associated with a feeder account.

National Savings products

National Savings products range from those that accept small savings to those that accept lump sums of up to £250,000. Some products enjoy generous tax concessions that make them especially attractive to higher rate taxpayers, while others pay income gross, which is convenient for non-taxpayers. The rates and range of the products frequently change, and you can get up-to-date information about what is on offer from post offices or from the Department for National Savings.

Bonds

A bond is a loan that you make to an organisation which you trust to pay you back. You lend the money, usually for a fixed number of years, and the borrower gives you a certificate promising to pay you back with interest. In the meantime, you can sell the bond certificate to someone else, depending on the type of bond – its market value will usually vary over time.

What's the difference between stocks and bonds?

Fixed-interest securities are normally called 'stocks' in the City of London, while equities are called 'shares'. In the USA, equities are called 'stocks', and fixed-interest securities are called 'bonds'. In this book I call fixed-interest securities 'bonds' and equities 'shares' – this is because much of the investment writing you read as you develop your skills comes from the USA, and the word 'stock' causes the most confusion. Don't worry about confusing your broker – he or she will know what you mean if you say 'bond'.

How safe are bonds?

It all depends on the organisation which has issued the bond. This is, at root, just common sense – who would you feel safest lending money to, the Treasury or Wondermousetrap plc, manufacturers of the latest in musical mousetraps who are borrowing in order to expand into the musical rat trap market?

When you buy a bond, the most important thing to be sure of is that you are going to get your money back. Unlike buying shares, you are not participating in potential future profits – you are simple lending money.

To help you decide how safe a bond is, there are various rating systems. The most famous systems are Standard and Poor's, and Moody's. These companies specialise in analysing most of the bond offerings across the globe to see how safe the bond will really be. Bond issuers may be governments, semi-governmental organisations such as county councils, or large companies; the credit rating agencies look at all of them with a beady eye and estimate the chances that a particular borrower will default.

The borrower's bonds are then given a rating. The very best rating a bond can have is AAA ('triple A'). Usually, bonds issued by the governments of rich countries such as the UK are considered to be 'risk free' – although everyone knows that nothing can be 100% risk free. To find out the rating of a particular bond, ask your broker or financial adviser.

For small investors in the UK, the safest bonds to buy are those issued by the Government; they are called 'gilts'. Another way to lend cash to the Government is by buying National Savings products.

The financial characteristics of bonds

Here is a summary of the features of high-quality bonds.

- High liquidity. This simply means that you can normally buy and sell the bonds very quickly – your money isn't tied up until the end of the life of the bond, except with certain products.

- A fixed interest rate. In a world of rapidly changing interest rates, it helps to be able to get a guaranteed rate of interest for a fixed number of years.
- Low risk. Bonds issued by the major governments have virtually no risk of default (which is when the bond issuer doesn't pay the money back).
- Low returns. All you can hope to gain from buying a bond is the interest, plus the chance of a small capital gain if you sell the bond in certain market conditions (there is, of course, the chance of a small capital loss as well). Bonds are essentially a place to keep money safe, not to make it grow.
- Vulnerability to inflation. If you keep a bond until it expires, inflation will have eaten away at its capital value. While the interest you receive may compensate for this, the longer the life of the bond, the more risk you are taking that inflation will outpace the value of the interest. The most extreme example of this are the infamous War Loans, which were issued during World War I, and cannot be redeemed unless the Government wishes to pay the money back.

The coupon

The interest you earn on a bond is normally paid twice a year, and is called 'the coupon'. You will see from the financial press that there is a wide range in the value of coupons on different bonds in issue, which show how much interest rates have varied over the years.

Yields

The 'current yield' on a bond is simply its annual rate of interest divided by its current market value. It is the way of working out the current value of a bond. If the market price of a bond falls, its yield rises, because the rate of return on capital increases, and, conversely, if the market price of a bond rises, its yield will fall.

EXAMPLE

Marcia buys a 10% bond with a face value of £100, but current interest rates have fallen to 9%, so she is asked to pay £111.11 for the bond. This is because the current yield of the bond has to match the interest rate an investor would currently get elsewhere. If the person selling the bond to Marcia asked £100 for it, Marcia would be getting a bargain, because she would be earning 1% more interest than the current rate.

The price of the bond is calculated by finding the sum that would generate the going rate of interest, which in this case is 9%.

0.09 of X = the coupon rate (10%)
X = 10 ÷ 0.09 = £111.11

If interest rates subsequently fall to 8%, Marcia will be able to sell her bond for £125:

0.08 of X = the coupon rate (10%)
X = 10 ÷ 0.08 = £125

Thus, Marcia will have made a capital gain of £125 – £111.11 = £13.89 on her bond.

This is the mechanism by which the price of a bond changes according to changes in current interest rates.

There are two other important 'yield' concepts which you will come across.

- Redemption yield
- Yield curve

The redemption yield

The redemption yield, or 'yield to maturity', is a measure used to compare different bonds. The redemption yield tries to measure the difference between the price you pay for the bond and what you will get for it when it matures. If you hold a bond for the rest of its life (until 'redemption'), you will make either a capital gain or a capital loss, as well as benefiting from the interest payments in the meantime. Working out a redemption yield accurately is complicated, so in practice investors simply look up the redemption yield for a bond in the *Financial Times*. Here's the general principle.

EXAMPLE

Marcia buys a 10% bond with a face value of £100 in the year 2001 for £111.11 because the current interest rate is 9%. The bond will be redeemed four years later in 2005 for £100. This means that she will make a capital loss if she holds it to redemption of £11.11, which is the difference between the face value of the bond and the price which she paid for it. Dividing this loss by the number of years left to run, we get:

$$11.11 \div 4 = £2.78$$

£2.78 is the amount of capital loss per year. Now she calculates what percentage £2.78 is of £111.11, the price she paid for the bond:

$$2.78 \div 111.11 = 0.025 = 2.5\%$$

At the time she buys the bond, interest rates are at 9%, so the current yield is:

$$\text{Coupon} \div \text{current price} \times 100$$
$$10 \div 111.11 \times 100 = 9$$

To work out approximately the redemption yield, Marcia subtracts her annual percentage of capital loss from the current yield:

$$9 - 2.5 = 6.5$$

This tells her that the redemption yield is 6.5%. The calculation is only approximate, though, because it doesn't take compound interest into account, so Marcia is wiser simply to look up the published redemption yield in the financial press.

Since the market value of her bond will fluctuate over the life of the bond in line with interest rates, the redemption yield only tells Marcia what will happen if she holds the bond to redemption – if, as in the previous example, interest rates fell to 8%, she would be able to sell the bond for a capital gain before the end of its life.

Comparing redemption yields

If you compare the redemption yields of different bonds which are at the same risk level, you will find that some are higher than others. This is because the longer a bond has to run, the higher its redemption yield will usually be as a reward for lending the money for a longer time. This brings us to the idea of the 'yield curve'.

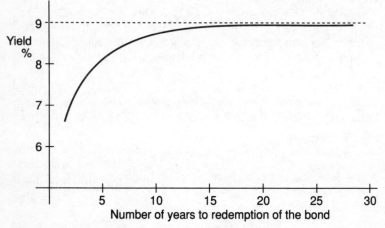

Figure 4.1 A normal yield curve

The yield curve

If you draw a graph of the redemption yields of bonds which are of comparable risk but have different lengths of time left to run, you will get a curved line, known as the 'yield curve'.

Figure 4.1 shows a 'normal' yield curve, where money lent for shorter periods of time earns less interest than money which is lent for longer. At certain times, however, bond prices behave differently, and there is an 'inverted' yield curve, as in Figure 4.2.

Inverted yield curves occur when there is a lot of uncertainty about future interest rates, and consequently buyers move in and out of bonds rapidly. These buyers are mainly banks and institutional investors; banks mainly buy short-term bonds (shorts), while the institutions tend to buy long-term ones ('longs'), leaving medium-term

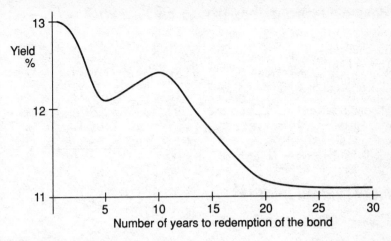

Figure 4.2 An inverted yield curve

bonds (5–15 years) out in the cold, which can cause them to have a better yield than longs. This can cause a 'hump' in the curve (see Figure 4.2) which reflects the unpopularity of medium-term bonds.

Since bond prices vary all the time, you will find that the yield curve varies also. Yields can easily fluctuate by 5% in a single year.

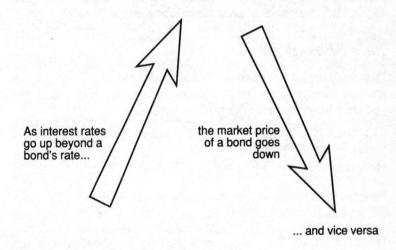

As interest rates go up beyond a bond's rate...

the market price of a bond goes down

... and vice versa

Figure 4.3 Interest rates and bond prices

Why do bond prices go up and down?

Between the time it is issued and the time it is redeemed, the price of a bond in the market varies. If you look in the day's *Financial Times*, you will find the current market price of any given bond, together with other data including its yields.

The main factor affecting the price is inflation, which drives interest rates generally. If interest rates go up beyond the bond's rate, the price of a bond goes down, and if interest rates go down below the bond's rate, the price of the bond will go up.

How to deal in gilts

You can buy and sell gilts in several ways.

● Through a broker
● By directly dealing with another private investor
● From some accountants and solicitors
● From the National Savings Stock Register (NSSR)

In general, the best way to buy is through the NSSR, because it charges very low commissions – when you buy, you pay £1 for the first £250, and 50p more per £125 above this, and when you sell you pay 10p per £10 up to £100, £1 for sales between £100 and £250, and £1 per £125 above this. Interest is paid gross, but is taxable.

Index-linked gilts

These pay a rate of interest linked to the official inflation figure. If you buy an index-linked gilt at face value and keep it to redemption you are guaranteed to make a profit in real terms.

The introduction of index-linked gilts has made it possible to measure the 'yield gap' between index-linked gilts and shares – if the overall yield on shares (see page 70) drops below the yield on index-linked gilts, it is a sign that share prices are too high, and that you should consider selling your shares and putting the money in gilts.

How the interest is paid

You usually get the interest twice a year. This means that when you buy a bond you need to know if the interest ('dividend') is close to being paid or has already been paid.

- About five weeks before the dividend is paid, the bond is said to be 'ex-dividend'. This means that the seller will keep the dividend which is coming.
- At other times a bond is 'cum dividend', meaning that you will get the next dividend.

Ex-dividend bonds are slightly cheaper to compensate for the loss of the next dividend payment.

————— Summary —————

The safest type of bond is almost certainly the gilt-edged stock issued by the UK Government, and this is where investors should begin their forays into bonds.

- In general, you should expect to get a slightly higher return on bonds than on other types of cash deposit, but less than you would get on shares. This reflects the relative level of risk of bonds as a class of investment.
- Most gilts have high liquidity – you can buy and sell them quickly and easily.
- There is no capital gains tax on gilts, which encourages speculation – if you buy a gilt, or any bond, and interest rates subsequently go down, the price of the bond will go up and you can take a tax-free capital gain if you wish.

5
SHARES

In this chapter we look at:

- What is a share?
- The stock exchange
- The London Stock Exchange
- Long-term rewards
- Characteristics of quoted shares as an investment
- How do you make money in shares?
- Approaches to direct investment in shares
- Dealing costs
- Summary for people who invest directly in shares
- Collective investments

What is a share?

In a limited company, whether it is private or a plc (public limited company), the ownership is organised in the form of shares. It is simple enough in principle – if three people, say, form a limited company and each put in £100, they might have the company issue 300 shares, and each take 100 of them. If a fourth person came along with money to invest, they might sell him or her some of their shares, or they might have the company issue more shares in return for the investment. There are many clever permutations in the share-issuing method, and each one may have a different effect on the ownership pattern and accounts of the company.

Shares are also called 'equities', and, to add to the confusion, in the USA they are called 'stocks'.

As well as the 'ordinary' share, which we will look at in this chapter, there are a number of other types of share, such as 'preference' shares, which are more complicated and are outside the scope of this book. An 'ordinary' share gives you the chance to make a profit or a loss when you sell it, and also the right to receive a share of the company's profits each year (the 'dividend'). You should bear in mind that it is the company's board which decides how much of its profits it is going to pay out in dividends; sometimes the directors will prefer to keep most of the profits within the company for the benefit of the business.

The stock exchange

The stock exchange is the essence of the capitalist system of financing industry. Here's how it works.

● All companies need money to grow, and one way of obtaining this money is to raise it from others by selling them shares.
● Most outside investors don't particularly like investing money in small companies, mainly because it is a lot of trouble to find out if they are worthwhile, and even if they are, it may not be easy to sell the shares later. In other words, investors want to know that their shares are liquid; the jargon term for this is good marketability.
● Since the last century, the massive expansion in trade and industry across the world has created vast companies employing thousands of people. These concerns need money, in the same way that a little company does, but they are more attractive to investors. This is because it is less trouble, in theory anyway, to find out about them. It is also easier to find buyers for their shares.
● This is where a stock exchange comes in – it is simply a market-place where people and organisations buy and sell shares in large companies.

There are many stock exchanges across the world, and some are a good deal more honest than others. The idea of stock exchanges has existed at least since the Middle Ages, at different times, in various parts of the world. Today, with the apparent collapse of capitalism's younger ideological rivals, the whole world seems to want to develop stock exchanges, and with the advent of information technology they are becoming increasingly interconnected. This is what is meant by the 'global marketplace'; it is a grand, optimistic idea that we are heading for a kind of giant stock exchange which all the countries of the world can participate in. The reality is somewhat different at present, as we will see in Chapter 9.

The London Stock Exchange

The London Stock Exchange is actually a collection of marketplaces dealing in different types of financial security, including shares, and is based in the City of London.

UK residents are fortunate to have the London Stock Exchange on their doorsteps; it is one of the three biggest stock markets in the world, the others being New York and Tokyo, and turns over huge amounts of business in foreign shares (more than 790 billion pounds' worth in 1995) as well as being the main centre for UK dealing in equities.

Long-term rewards

Various studies have shown that holding good-quality shares over the long term, and reinvesting their dividends, has produced a better return than other classes of investment – about 7% before tax in real terms since the end of World War I. However, as the economist J.M. Keynes famously remarked, 'in the long run we are all dead'; we actually want to be able to enjoy some of these returns in our own lifetimes, so our returns may be less than this, and we may even lose money.

Characteristics of quoted shares as an investment

'Quoted' shares are simply shares which you can buy and sell in the stock market. The companies who are listed on the exchange are not all the same, so you have to pick and choose your shares carefully. The better quality shares have the following characteristics as an investment.

- High volatility – the price of a share can rise and fall dramatically over the course of a day.
- Liquidity – you can buy and sell good-quality shares quickly and easily.
- Relatively high risk – you don't know if the price of a share will go up, down or remain the same, or if the dividends you are paid will be regular. A company may go bust, or suddenly be downgraded.
- Some inflation protection in the long term – this has been true in the past, but it may not always hold true.

If you buy a share, you become a part owner in a company, and, in the case of ordinary shares, you have the right to share in its profits, vote on major issues affecting the company, and to attend its annual general meetings and ask question. Big companies have millions of shares issued, so as a small shareholder you will be one tiny voice amongst many. There are many regulations governing how a company's executives should behave towards its shareholders, but there is always the nagging doubt that smaller shareholders aren't treated very seriously – this varies from company to company.

Bull and bear markets

Although the average return on shares may have gone up overall in the long term, there seem to be shorter cycles when either most shares are going up in price (a bull market) or down in price (a bear market). During the first half of the 1990s we have seen a bull market, with many shares producing above-average returns; this suggests that we may be in for a bear market, but nobody knows when or if this will occur.

How do you make money in shares?

One of the most interesting and enjoyable things about the stock market is that there is no absolutely proven theory about how market prices behave. Academics and professionals argue incessantly about various methods, and new theories are developing all the time. Here we look at three important theories.

- The efficient market
- Fundamental analysis
- Technical analysis

The efficient market

This theory is more popular amongst academics than it is amongst practitioners, perhaps because it suggests a fairly cautious investment policy. It is connected with Modern Portfolio Theory (MPT) which was discussed in Chapter 1.

The idea is that there are so many clever professionals analysing all the information about quoted companies all the time that their actions cancel each other out, and that a private investor could do as well by throwing darts at a list of shares as he might by picking the shares on the advice of professionals. (You can see why many professionals aren't keen on this idea!) Efficient marketeers tell us that we should only pick shares on the basis of their risk – the big, massively capitalised companies being inherently less risky than the smaller ones – and spread our money between a collection of them. The market is 'efficient', they say, in the sense that the collective expertise of the professionals efficiently adjusts the prices of shares as soon as each new piece of information emerges which may affect their price. The price is 'adjusted' simply by the supply and demand effect of people buying and selling shares.

Fundamental analysis

Fundamental analysis looks at the companies themselves, and, amongst the purists, ignores short-term price fluctuations of the shares. An analyst will study what is happening in a particular industrial sector, and try to identify future trends in the business. Then he or she will take a particular company and go through its accounts with a fine-toothed comb, visit its premises, interview its executives and talk to its competitors, suppliers and customers. Back at the office, the analyst will continue to study other factors which may affect the future of the company, such as world oil prices and forthcoming political events. Every new piece of information will be noted and judged in the light of what is already known.

This type of analyst is doing a very thorough and professional job in trying to find out everything possible about a company. To do this properly, you have to specialise in only a few companies, so there are thousands of analysts employed in the City. Some are good, and some are not so good, as one might expect. If you become actively interested in owning shares, you will get to know some analysts; they can be extremely interesting to talk to about what is going on in a particular company, and you will quickly realise that, short of becoming an analyst yourself, you are unlikely to be able to find out as much information on your own.

The object of fundamental analysis is to make an informed guess about the true worth of a company; if the share price is lower than this valuation, then it makes sense, they say, to buy its shares because eventually the price will go up to reflect the true value, and you will make a profit.

Technical analysis

Technical analysis is easy to mock – the more extreme believers are called 'chartists' – because it ignores the underlying company and events in the 'real world' altogether. The theory is based on the insight that the 'smart money' (the big-time stock market players) know more than the rest of the investors, but that the rest follow where the smart money goes.

EXAMPLE

100 years ago the US stock markets were less regulated than they are now, and there were a number of big-time players, rejoicing in names like 'Diamond Jim' Brady and 'Bet a million' Gates, who could manipulate the market by buying the shares of one company heavily, and waiting for the price to go up. In certain conditions, many other investors would see the price going up and all pile in, in the expectation that it would continue to rise. The big player would then quietly sell out at a profit, and after a while other investors would begin to wonder why they had bought the shares in the first place. These people would then sell out, and then, finally, the thousands of

---

ill-informed small investors would get bored and begin to sell. By this time the share price would start to drop, causing more and more people to sell in a panic, which would make the share price drop even further. Sometimes the big player would then start buying again, causing another boom in the share price!

This phenomenon is known as 'investor psychology'. What technical analysts have done is to develop hugely complicated pseudo-theories about the patterns that price movements make. They claim to be able to spot particular shapes forming in the charts of share price movements, and thus predict where the share price is going to go next.

It all sounds a little mad, perhaps, but large banks and other financial institutions do pay large salaries to technical analysts. You should notice, though, that technical analysis is really about predicting very short-term changes in share prices, so if you take the private investor's costs of buying and selling into account, you will have to do considerably better using technical analysis than you would using fundamental analysis, which doesn't require you to buy and sell all the time.

You should also be aware that many, many serious mathematical studies of share price movements have found no real evidence that the technical analysts' patterns are really predictable.

Why you can be successful with a false theory

There are many other theories about how to predict share prices; recently the use of astrology has received some publicity, for example. Usually, the promoters of the theory will have some examples of their success to back up their claims – it would be silly not to, after all, if you wanted anyone to believe in your theory. But success in itself proves nothing, since you may simply have been lucky. There is nothing magical about this kind of luck; you can describe it mathematically using probability theory.

EXAMPLE

Kim and Helen have a drink in a bar every evening after work, and they always flip a coin to decide who will pay. The first time they play, they each have a 50/50 chance of winning. This is true for each time they play the game.

If they do this over several years, one of them will have won much more often (let's say it is Kim), because you get long 'runs' when the coin repeatedly comes up on one side. Kim's success is simply the result of chance, but it is very easy for the two friends to believe that there is some hidden reason behind her luck. They can then 'prove' their theory by pointing to the fact that Kim has won most of the time.

The same is true for some successful investors who take big risks in the stock market – they may have excellent results for no other reason than a series of chance events. It is only human to try to find a reason for one's luck, so such investors may honestly believe that they are using some special technique that actually has no foundation. If they are really lucky, they will then decide to retire from the market and keep their cash!

Approaches to direct investment in shares

If you are going to invest directly in shares, rather than using a collective fund (see page 71), you are embarking on what can easily become a lifetime of study. As your understanding of the markets and business grows, you will be able to take risks that would be unsafe when you are a novice. This isn't everyone's cup of tea, but for many people it becomes a very rewarding activity, not only in financial terms but also in terms of your development as a skilled investor.

As a non-professional, there are two basic approaches you can take.

1 Medium to long-term investing
2 Trading

Medium to long-term investing

This method relies mainly on fundamental analysis strategies, a popular form of which is known as 'value investing'.

Value investors believe that:

- you can assess a company's real value by studying its financial attributes. To do this you need to be fairly numerate and have a good grounding in basic accounting
- the price of a share does not usually reflect the company's true value
- eventually the share price will come to reflect the company's true value for a period

The gurus of value investing are Benjamin Graham and his student Warren Buffet, an American who has built up a personal fortune estimated at over $8 billion through investing in equities. See the Bibliography for their books.

Value investors essentially try to find companies which they value at more than their current share price; when they find them, they buy them and hang on to them for the medium to long term in the hope of getting exceptional returns.

A very important point to remember is that you don't need to get exceptional or above-average returns to do well as a long-term investor; as long as you achieve an average return, and the average returns of the stock market grow more, in real terms, than fixed-interest investments or property do during the same period, you will have achieved substantial growth to your capital.

- To achieve this growth, you should always reinvest your dividends, though not necessarily in the same shares.
- A good way to invest for the long term if you are a taxpayer is to use a PEP. This is discussed in Chapter 6.

Trading

An investor who 'trades' is one who buys and sells shares for a quick profit. This costs a good deal of money in taxes and commissions, and is much more risky than long-term investing.

Some traders buy and sell every day, but this is inadvisable unless you have nothing else to do except watch share prices. Others buy and sell less frequently – say once a week, or once a month – and often they act on the advice of their brokers.

Brokers love investors who trade; they make a commission every time their client buys or sells a share, irrespective of whether the client makes a loss or a profit. Investors who only buy a share once or twice a year and won't budge are pretty boring as far as brokers are concerned, although they may have some grudging respect for them.

Stockbrokers' services

Brokers offer two main types of service.

1 The full advisory service. If you don't have very much money to invest, your choice of brokers offering this service is relatively limited – some won't touch private clients who have less than a million pounds to play with. This is because under this scheme the broker agrees to advise you on individual shares and to discuss investment in general – you may talk to each other every day, so it has to be worth the broker's time to deal with you. You can expect to pay them a minimum of £25 each time you buy or sell shares – the average commission is 1.85% for 'bargains' (transactions) under £10,000.
2 The execution only service. This is a cheaper way to deal in shares; commissions are around 1% for bargains under £10,000, with a minimum of £9 per bargain. The regulations do not allow the staff who take your orders to give you advice of any kind. This actually causes more problems than you might expect, because if you are not familiar with all the technicalities you can make expensive mistakes.

EXAMPLE

Naomi has 100,000 shares with a face value of 1p in XYZ plc. The company has millions of shares in issue and decides to consolidate them by converting them into a smaller number of shares at a ratio of 100:1. Naomi now owns 1,000 shares with a face value of £1.

XYZ then decides to have a 'rights issue', which means that it offers its existing shareholders the rights to buy more shares; it does this to raise more money for the business. Let's suppose that Naomi is preoccupied with other matters and does not pay any attention to this offer.

XYZ now decides to consolidate its shares again, and Naomi ends up with, say 400 shares with a face value of £2.50. Her total shareholding is still worth £1,000, but she owns fewer shares.

Naomi decides to sell her shares, but still thinks she owns 100,000 of them. She telephones her execution-only broker and orders the sale of 100,000 XYZ. The broking staff are not obliged to remind her of the changes described, although a conscientious broking firm will do so, so Naomi may end up selling the 400 shares she owns plus 99,600 shares she doesn't own. She will then have to buy 99,600 shares in order to settle the account, which will cost her money in dealing costs, plus there is the risk that the share price has changed in the meantime. A very expensive mistake! If she had used a full advisory service, however, she would have redress against the broker if this mistake occurred.

Despite this horror story, you shouldn't feel that execution-only services are definitely not for you – just make sure that you are up to date with what is going on with the companies you invest in. You can do this by following the financial press (see the Bibliography) and carefully reading any documents sent to you by the company.

There is one other service that some brokers offer, called the discretionary service. This is normally only available to people with fairly large sums to invest; you simply leave all the decisions to your broker, who buys and sells as he or she thinks fit, according to a basic strategy you have agreed at the outset. A good broker can be expected to do this conscientiously. Beware the faceless corporations, though – they may well produce below-average returns if you give them their head.

Dealing costs

Unless a company is being brought to the stock market for the first time, as was the case with the privatisations of nationalised industries such as gas and water, you will usually have to buy shares through a broker. In addition to the broker's commission, there are other costs.

- Stamp duty of 0.5% on purchases. This is due to be abolished when paperless trading is introduced.
- The bid/offer spread. Share prices have two prices, the price at which you can buy them (the offer) and the price at which you can sell them (the bid). The difference between the two prices is known as the bid/offer spread, and is a profit taken by the 'market maker', a specialist firm at the heart of the stock market system. Bid/offer spreads vary greatly; a rule of thumb is that the bigger and more popular a company is, the narrower the bid/offer spread will be, and thus the cheaper it will be to deal in the shares.

As has been mentioned before, the total cost of dealing makes the constant buying and selling of shares quite expensive. This may not matter if you are making profits, but it does have an adverse effect on your returns. Another way of looking at costs is to compare them with the costs of buying and selling houses, which are also high, and become a disincentive to buy and sell at low profit.

P/e ratios

The price/earnings ratio, or p/e ratio, is a useful measurement of a share. It gives you a figure for the ratio between the current after-tax earnings of a company and its share price, so it tells you how much the stock market thinks that the company is worth at the moment. Normally the p/e will be a number between 5 and 25; if the p/e is, say, ten, it means that the price you are paying for a share represents ten years' worth of the company's current after-tax earnings.

- Very high p/es – say, over 20 – mean that the market expects the company to increase its after-tax earnings rapidly in future years.
- Very low p/es – five or less – mean that the market expects the company's after-tax earnings to decline rapidly in future years, and possibly even that the company may go bust.

Long-term investors usually think that buying shares with lowish p/es, say between 7 and 12, is a good idea if they also expect that the company's earnings will start to grow in future years. You can find the p/es of shares in the share listings of the *Financial Times*.

Yield

The yield on a share is the annual dividend paid last year divided by the current market price of the share. Yields therefore go up and down according to the share price. They are a useful measurement because you can use them to compare the income return you will get from a share with that from other shares, or even other investments, such as bonds. What they don't tell you, though, is how much next year's dividend will be, or even if it will be paid at all. Nor do yields tell you anything about whether the share price will go up or down. Shares with a high yield are thought to have an above-average risk.

Stock indices

A stock index is a measurement of how a certain group of shares is performing. You can use this to see how a particular share or another group of shares is doing. Here are some of the important indices for the London Stock Exchange.

- FTSE100 (the *Financial Times* Stock Exchange 100 Share Index). This measures 100 of the largest companies quoted in London, and is known as the 'Footsie'.
- FT-30 Share Index, (the Financial Times Ordinary Share Index). This measures 30 of the largest companies quoted on the London Stock Exchange.
- The FT Actuaries indices. These measure the performances of different industrial sectors so you can compare how, say, textiles are doing against shipping.
- The FT-Actuaries All-Share Index. This measures the top 800 or so companies on the exchange, and contains the largest number of companies of all the various indices.

When people talk about the 'average' performance of the stock market, they are usually talking about how one of the indices has performed. The great game of the market is to beat the average, but as long as the average gives you good long-term real returns, you have nothing to worry about if you are only getting an average return.

Summary for people who invest directly in shares

It is perfectly legal for you to rush out tomorrow and start to buy and sell shares, and if you are in a bull market you may make money – even if you are an amateur astrologer. If you are intrigued by the whole thing, and you are spending money you can easily afford to lose, one could even say that this is not a bad way to learn the game. Most people, though, would prefer to learn rather more about how the market works before jumping in! If you do want to become a direct investor, try spending a year reading stock market books and the financial press before you actually start buying; the more you learn, the better your chances of a reasonably good result.

Collective investments

Many people take their time before investing directly, and if you are one of them, or if you simply don't want the aggravation of learning all about the market and business in general, you can still participate in the market through collective investments. The two main kinds are:

1 unit trusts
2 investment trusts

The basic idea behind both of them is that a lot of private people put money into a fund and leave it to professional managers to invest the money for them. This takes all the hassle and worry out of the investment – in theory, anyway. Strictly speaking, pension funds and insurance company funds are also collective investments, since they are collections of money from lots of private individuals professionally invested in the stock market and elsewhere.

You pay a price when you put money into a collective investment because you have to pay for these professionals' work as well as, indirectly, having to pay for the dealing costs outlined on pages 68–9. Unit trusts in particular have become heavily marketed consumer products, and many of them do not give you good value.

In addition, not all collective investments perform well, despite the fact that they are run by professionals. If you look in the *Financial Times* on a Saturday, you will see that some collective investment funds have lost substantial amounts of capital in only a few years. As always, of course, the past performance of an investment does not tell you how it will perform in the future.

Unit trusts

Unit trusts give you 'units' in the fund in return for your money. The fund itself will be invested in shares, bonds and other investments, and you will be given information on the strategy and type of investments of a particular unit trust before you buy.

The arguments in favour of units trusts are:

- they may give you better diversification than you can get on your own
- they require less of your attention than direct investment
- they are well regulated

Unit trusts are a form of trust, unlike investment trusts which are limited companies.

Types of unit trust

There are 22 different categories of unit trusts. The main ones are as follows.

- UK balanced – these try to produce returns that follow the FT-Actuaries All-Share Index.
- UK equity income – these aim to produce a growing level of income if you hold the units for several years. Initially the income will be less than you could get by depositing cash.
- UK growth – these try to obtain capital growth, so yields (see page 70) will be low.
- Offshore trusts – this means that they are not 'authorised unit trusts' in the UK. Many of them are run from places like the Channel Islands. They are harder to buy and sell in the UK, and may be less well regulated, so you should check them carefully before investing. Their charges tend to be even higher than normal.

There are 'green' and 'ethical' unit trusts, packaged to appeal to consumers who are passionate about these issues.

Saving

Many unit trusts let you save small sums each month, and even miss out a few months. This is quite a good way to save, and should normally produce better returns than insurance-based saving schemes.

Unit trust charges

There is no doubt that unit trusts have relatively high charges; you will usually pay:

- a bid/offer spread on the price of units when you buy and sell – the spread can be as high as 13.5% in certain circumstances
- an annual management fee, which is not usually more than 1%
- a 'front-end load', which is a fee charged when you first buy your units – it can be as much as 5% of the money you invest

Dealing in unit trusts

Unit trusts are very widely available – you can buy them from press advertisements and through many outlets in the high street.

Choosing a unit trust

There are over 1,300 unit trusts available in the UK, managed by nearly 200 management groups. With such a bewildering choice, you will need some help.

- Unit trust advisory services (UTAS) monitor most of the unit trusts; you can get detailed reports from them on the ones you are interested in. Often the first report you request is free.
- Magazines such as the *Investor's Chronicle* provide useful information and comment on unit trusts.

As a general rule, don't be too impressed by fancy gimmicks – decide on how much risk you want to take, and whether you want to stick to capital growth or income. This will narrow the field somewhat!

Investment trusts

Unlike unit trusts, investment trusts are actually public limited companies which are quoted on the stock exchange. Instead of buying units, you are actually buying shares in the company. The business of the company is simply to invest on behalf of its shareholders. As with unit trusts, there are a large number of categories to choose from, and many of them operate savings schemes for small investors. Other than an annual management charge of about half a percent, there are no other fees or 'front end loads'.

The arguments in favour of investment trusts over unit trusts are as follows.

- The rules allow investment trusts to borrow money, which means that they can use gearing to their advantage, unlike unit trusts. This makes them slightly more risky than unit trusts, and offers a slightly better chance of getting a better return.
- The value of the assets of an investment trust is often slightly more than the price of its shares.

EXAMPLE

XYZ investment trust has a current share price of, say, 90p. Its assets are £10 million, and there are 10 million shares in issue. This means when you buy one share, you are buying one 10 millionth of its assets of £10 million, which is £1 – this is called its net asset value (NAV) per share. Since you can buy a share for 90p, you are getting a bargain on the NAV.

Choosing an investment trust

The Association of Investment Trust Companies (see Useful Addresses) publishes useful details about 311 investment trust companies which will help you to narrow down your choice. You will notice that some investment trust companies are based in Scotland, which has a long and honourable tradition of careful financial management.

You can buy shares directly from the investment trust itself, which is usually the cheapest way, or you can buy them through a broker or other intermediary.

Summary of collective investments

- If you want to dip your toe in the water of the stock market before plunging in, it makes sense to invest in a unit trust or an investment trust.
- Make sure you study the literature and any reports you can get carefully before you invest. Watch out for high charges.
- Remember that all collective investments can go down as well as up.
- It may take you a little more trouble to find an investment trust than it would to find a unit trust, but the effort may well be worth it in terms of the returns you get.

6

PERSONAL EQUITY PLANS (PEPS)

PEPs are a tax-incentive scheme for UK taxpayers; if you are not a taxpayer you do not need a PEP. In this chapter we look at:

- Personal equity plans (PEPs)
- The government's PEP rules
- PEPs as a long-term strategy
- Special rules for unit trusts and investment trusts
- Saving through a PEP
- Managed PEPs versus self-select PEPs
- The charges
- Single company PEPs (SCPs)
- Corporate bonds through a PEP
- Cash and General PEPs

—— Personal equity plans (PEPs) ——

PEPs were brought in by the government in 1986 to encourage more people to buy shares. It was part of government policy, and still is, to introduce new generations to the stock market. During the 1960s and 1970s, the number of private shareholders dropped drastically, due in large part to extremely heavy rates of tax on profits and investments in general during that period. In addition, the industrial unrest of the 1970s made buying shares in large companies seem singularly un-attractive to many people, and by 1979 it was virtually impossible to find a broker who would act for you unless you were very rich; either you bought unit trusts or investment trusts, or you stayed out of the market.

Individuals' savings were still going into the stock market in the form of pension funds and insurance-based schemes which are controlled by vastly powerful organisations known as the 'institutions'. The institutions became, and still are, the most powerful investors in the markets.

When PEPS were first brought in, no-one paid much attention to them because the rules were so complicated and expensive to administer that the financial services industry didn't want to bother with them and the public couldn't see much of a benefit in using them.

Gradually the scheme has been broadened and simplified, and PEPs now represent an excellent way of medium- to long-term investing. There is now more than 15 billion pounds' worth of private investors' money invested through PEPs in the UK, and this figure is still growing.

Unfortunately, the success of PEPs has meant that, as with the unit trust industry, there is now a proliferation of PEP schemes which are aggressively marketed to consumers but offer poor value – PEP schemes are not all alike! You will need to shop around to find the kind of PEP which is best suited to your own particular circumstances.

The government's PEP rules

The aggressive marketing of some PEP schemes has created a good deal of confusion over the rules. This is because the firm providing a PEP is allowed to add on its own restrictions if it wishes to do so.

The government's rules for PEPs are as follows.

- There is no income tax or capital gains tax on investments held through a PEP.
- You can invest up to £6,000 a year in a General PEP, and a further £3,000 a year in a Single Company PEP (SCP).
- Anyone who is over 18 and is resident and ordinarily resident (see page 173) in the UK can take out a PEP. If you become non-resident you can keep the PEPs you already have, but you can't take out any more.

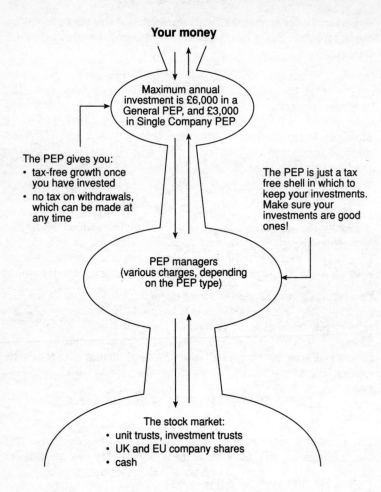

Your money

Maximum annual investment is £6,000 in a General PEP, and £3,000 in Single Company PEP

The PEP gives you:
- tax-free growth once you have invested
- no tax on withdrawals, which can be made at any time

The PEP is just a tax free shell in which to keep your investments. Make sure your investments are good ones!

PEP managers (various charges, depending on the PEP type)

The stock market:
- unit trusts, investment trusts
- UK and EU company shares
- cash

Figure 6.1 The PEP principle

- You can invest in any of the following:
  - UK shares quoted on the stock market
  - European Community shares quoted on EU markets
  - UK company bonds, preference shares and convertibles
  - cash
  - UK investment trusts
  - UK unit trusts

- A year, for the purposes of PEP allowances, is the tax year which runs from the 6th of April in one year to the 5th of April in the next.

—— PEPs as a long-term strategy ——

Most people are unlikely to save more than £9,000 a year for investment in bonds and equities, so a PEP scheme may be all you ever need for this type of investment. It is important, though, to remember that a PEP is only a tax-free container, or 'vehicle', for your investments; your focus must still be on selecting investments which give you good diversification and adequate returns for the level of risk you are willing to take.

EXAMPLE

Jane and Hugh are high earners in their thirties; they each take out a General PEP and a Single Company PEP and contribute the maximum allowed each year for ten years. We are assuming that future governments will not abolish PEPs.

Taking their two PEPs together, their combined contributions are £18,000 a year. Using the future value formula (see page 15):

$$FV = [p \times < (1 + i)^n - 1>] \div i$$

where p is the amount invested per period, n is the number of periods and i is the rate of interest per period, and assuming a conservative real return of 5% a year

$$
\begin{aligned}
FV &= [18,000 \times < (1 + 0.05)^{10} - 1>] \div 0.05 \\
&= [18,000 \times < 1.05^{10} - 1>] \div 0.05 \\
&= [18,000 \times < 1.63 - 1>] \div 0.05 \\
&= [18,000 \times 0.63] \div 0.05 \\
&= 11,340 \div 0.05 \\
&= 226,800
\end{aligned}
$$

Now let's assume that Jane and Hugh cease to contribute to their PEPs, but keep the PEP fund they have already accumulated.

Applying the rule of 115 we see that at a real rate of return of 5%

$115 \div 5 = 23$

it will take 23 more years for their fund to have trebled to £680,400. This is a tax-free capital sum based on total savings of £180,000 over ten years.

Thus, by the time Jane and Hugh are retiring, they will have a substantial sum available to them in addition to their pensions and other assets; what's more, they could have withdrawn money at any time during the period or even borrowed against the fund. Of course, if PEPs are allowed to continue in their present form for three decades or more, and Jane and Hugh are able to make the maximum contributions each year, the fund would be even larger.

As always, remember that equity-based investments are not risk free – they can go down as well as up!

Special rules for unit trusts and investment trusts

Under PEP rules, unit trusts and investment trusts are either 'qualifying' or 'non-qualifying'.

- Qualifying unit trusts and investment trusts (QITs) are those that have more than 50% of their assets invested in UK and EU securities. You can invest in them only through a General PEP and you can only use up to £3,000 of your £6,000 allowance on them each year.
- Non-qualifying unit trusts and investment trusts (NQITs) are those that have less than 50% invested in UK and EU securities. You can only invest in them through a General PEP and you are restricted to a maximum of £1,500 of your annual allowance. Don't dismiss them out of hand, though, since some of these funds are investing in fast-growing markets abroad.

The rules allow you to hold QITs and NQITs together in the same PEP, and use the rest of your allowance on other qualifying investments.

Saving through a PEP

Many PEP providers will allow you to save regular or irregular sums through a PEP, which makes them well suited to self-employed people who have irregular incomes. Investing in shares in this way has the effect of averaging out the price you are paying for shares, which protects you to some degree from share price volatility.

Managed PEPs versus self-select PEPs

Managed PEPs are those where the PEP provider decides on your investments for you. Self-select PEPs are those which allow you to choose your investments yourself, normally from a range of securities decided on by the provider. Either type may or may not be cost-effective, depending on their charges and rules.

The charges

Charges vary widely between PEP providers, and will depend in part on how much work you want them to do and how often you switch your investments around. Here are some typical good-value charges:

- purchase – £5 flat fee, plus 0.15% broker's commission
- sales – £20, plus 0.23% broker's commission
- transferring investments in or out of a PEP – £10.50
- withdrawals of cash – £10
- transferring investments from another PEP provider – £30 plus £15 per shareholding
- transferring investments to another PEP provider – £50 plus £10.50 per shareholding
- valuations and extra statements, other than the annual valuation and statement – £5
- attending shareholder's meeting and voting – £30

You will find that some PEP providers have much higher charges than this, so shop around!

It is a good idea not to switch providers each year if you have found one which you are happy with. Although you are entitled to have a separate General PEP each year with a different provider, this is likely to lead to a haphazard collection of investments which will be awkward to manage and expensive in terms of charges.

— Single company PEPs (SCPs) —

Unless you can afford to put away the maximum £6,000 a year in a General PEP, then an SCP is not for you. The reasons are simple.

- An SCP in any particular year has to hold the shares of one company only.
- If you have more than 10% of your total shareholdings in a single company you are probably not well diversified – if the shares in that company do badly, it will affect the performance of your entire investment in shares.

SCPs have two main functions.

- The first is for employees of the company concerned, who may be offered extra incentives to hold their company's shares through an SCP. This kind of PEP scheme will be backed by the company itself, and will be designed for the money to buy the same company's shares each year.
- The second is for everyone else who wants to maximise the amount of money they can put into PEPs each year. You may well want to use your £3,000 on a different company each year. If this is the case, you should seek a PEP provider who is willing to let you do this with few restrictions.

If you are contemplating using an SCP, you are safer buying shares in one of the top 100 companies (as listed in the FTSE 100) than buying those of a smaller and less well-known company. This should reduce the risk and volatility of your holding.

— Corporate bonds through a PEP —

If you weren't going to invest in corporate bonds before the PEP rules were changed in 1995 to include them, why would you invest in them now? They are quite a lot riskier than gilts, so for the less experienced investor they are probably not a good idea.

A large number of corporate bond PEP schemes have been created since the change in the rules, and while some have useful advantages, you must avoid the 'fear trap'.

EXAMPLE

David is middle-aged, but he's an inexperienced investor. He is afraid of shares, and he is afraid of inflation. The most important thing on his mind is not losing his capital. For many years he buys short gilts and gets a poor real return – sometimes it is even a negative real return. After a while he gets fed up with this, and looks for ways of getting a better return. He sticks to bonds, because he has got it into his head that only bonds will do.

He doesn't distinguish between the levels of risk inherent in different bonds, but concentrates on getting the best rate possible. The only way of getting the best rate possible is to increase your risk. If David invests in a corporate bond, he is taking the risk that the company may fall on hard times and stop paying the interest on the bond for a few years; this will adversely affect the market price of the bond. If this happens, David will have had all the misery of losing money in the stock market without any of the fun of getting really good returns. In other words, when examining individual corporate bonds you should try to assess whether the risk of loss outweighs the extra few per cent, or fractions of a per cent, that corporate bonds offer.

For knowledgeable investors, however, the freedom to invest in corporate bonds with maturity dates of over five years through a PEP, as well as more rarified securities such as debentures and convertibles, is desirable. Once you know enough to 'take a view' about the market at any particular time, you will want the freedom to move in and out of bonds and equities without incurring tax problems, and this is what PEPs now allow you to do.

Cash and General PEPs

The PEP rules say that you can only hold cash in a General PEP for the purpose of investment in qualifying investments. This is ambiguous, since the Inland Revenue has not made any clear statements about how this is to be defined, except for saying that you can't hold cash in a PEP for the primary purpose of avoiding paying income tax on the interest you earn from a cash deposit. As the rules stand, it appears that you can put cash into a General PEP and leave it there indefinitely, so long as you intend to invest it in qualifying investments one day, even if that day is many years from now.

If a lot of people start to exploit this loophole simply to use their General PEPs as a way of holding cash in the long term, it is possible that the rules will be tightened up. As long as you do genuinely intend to use the cash to invest in qualifying investments, though, you should have nothing to worry about.

Another point worth bearing in mind is that if you decide to get out of shares and bonds for a period because you don't like the way the market is going, you can sell them for cash, still keep the cash in the PEP, and reinvest when you think the markets are improving.

Summary

PEPs are an extremely attractive tax incentive for UK taxpayers, and now offer a great deal of flexibility. You can cash in part or all of your PEP at any time, and you should get improved long-term returns because of the tax-free growth.

- As well as the tax advantages, there is also the benefit that the paperwork is considerably reduced – the PEP manager will do much of it for you.
- Shop around carefully before choosing your PEP provider; essentially you should be looking for the maximum flexibility at the lowest possible cost.
- The costs of running a PEP mean that it only really becomes cost-effective if you hold a PEP for more than seven years or so. It is not a good idea to use a PEP if you think you are going to need to cash it in sooner than this.

- Elections are looming, and it may be that a future government alters the PEP rules, so don't assume that you will be able to invest in PEPs each year for the next 30 or 40 years. The PEPs you already have should be safe, though, because it is unlikely, even if new PEPs are abolished, for new legislation to be applied retroactively to existing PEPs.

7

DERIVATIVES

Derivatives are a group of sophisticated 'paper' contracts which are derived from real assets such as shares and bonds. While they do have some sober uses, you should avoid them until, or unless, you are willing to take the extreme risks that go with these highly volatile investments. In this chapter we will look at:

- Commodities
- Financial futures
- The London International Financial Futures and Options Exchange (LIFFE)
- Options
- Traded options
- Warrants

Commodities

Strictly speaking, commodities are not themselves derivatives, but 'commodity futures' are. Commodities are simply the basic products such as oil, tin, gold, wheat, zinc, pork bellies, coffee and sugar that are produced, traded and processed all over the world. Commodities play a fundamental part in the world's economy; if you remember the chaos in 1973 when the OPEC oil cartel suddenly decided to raise oil prices, you will see just how quickly a hiccup in commodity prices can lead to economic mayhem across the globe.

The businesses that produce commodities are vulnerable to many factors beyond their control. Suppose, for instance, you are a wheat producers who has just had a bumper harvest. Terrific! You should be able to sell much more wheat than usual and make more money – but if all the other wheat producers have got extra wheat to sell too, the market will be flooded and the buyers won't want to pay so much for the wheat. Furthermore, a gang of big-time wheat producers might try to get in first and bully a lot of the buyers to buy their wheat, leaving the other producers in an even worse state.

Wars, strikes, unseasonal weather, changes in consumer tastes, plagues of insects, leaf diseases and a host of other factors all make world commodity prices volatile – that is, producers never really know what price they will get next year, or even next month, for their goods. This makes it hard for them to run their businesses, so they need some way to insure against future price changes. This is done by trading in 'commodity futures'.

Commodity futures

Suppose our wheat producer wants to make sure that he can sell 100 tons of wheat at price X next year. He knows that if he's lucky he might get more for the wheat next year, but conversely he might get less for it. He makes a deal with a buyer to deliver the 100 tons of wheat at a fixed date in the future for price X. This is known as a 'futures contract'. This kind of arrangement suits both sides because it helps to take some of the uncertainty out of their businesses – they are hedging their bets, and in the financial markets this technique is still called 'hedging'.

A third kind of dealer now appears in the market. This is the speculator, who isn't interested in producing or buying the commodity, but only in making a profit out of the difference in price between a futures contract and the actual market price at the time the commodity is delivered.

The hedgers are seeking to reduce the volatility of their operations, while the speculators are gambling on price movements, and must watch the market fluctuations like hawks.

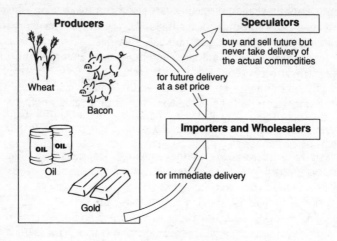

Figure 7.1 Commodities and commodity futures

Financial futures

In the last few decades, the idea behind futures contracts has been extended to cover shares, bonds, currencies and interest rates. In these cases, the 'producers' and 'buyers' are mainly banks, who want to hedge, and the speculators are anyone else who is willing to take a gamble – perhaps not surprisingly banks have been known to become speculators too.

The attraction of financial futures for speculators lies in the fact that they have to put very little money down (called 'the margin') when they make a bet. This is an example of 'high gearing'. It all sounds very exciting, but it is really only a game for professionals, and even they get it wrong. Recent derivatives disasters include Orange County, a local authority in California, going bust after some bad bets, and Metalgesellschaft, a large German corporation, losing a massive fortune in derivative trading. Nearer home, it is said that Nick Leeson could not have brought Barings, Britain's oldest merchant bank, to its knees if the extraordinary complexity of his derivatives deals had not made it difficult for his superiors to understand what was going on.

Here is a simplified example to illustrate the point.

EXAMPLE

Jed is a big-time speculator who decides to buy £5 million worth of futures contracts. He only has to put up a small proportion of that money as a deposit – say it is as little as £50,000, or 1%. If he guesses right, and makes, say, 10% on the gamble, he receives half a million pounds for an outlay of a mere £50,000. If he has got it wrong and loses by 10%, he has lost his £50,000, plus a further £450,000 which he must pay as soon as it is due.

The London International Financial Futures and Options Exchange (LIFFE)

The great centre for futures trading is in Chicago. For an amusing account of what it is like to be a trader there, read *Trading Rules* by William Eng (see Bibliography) – it will help you to appreciate just how fierce the futures world really is.

In the UK, LIFFE (pronounced 'life'), is the market place for dealing in financial futures and options, and is the third largest in the world. They run a number of useful courses for private investors who want to learn more about the arcane world of derivatives (see Useful Addresses).

LIFFE is one of the last places which uses the 'open outcry' system – traders congregate in 'pits', using a complex system of hand signals as well as their voices to make as many deals as they can in the shortest possible time. To an outsider, this looks like a madhouse of screaming, gesticulating lunatics, but it is in fact a highly efficient system of rapid trading.

In order to trade on LIFFE, you need to have a broker who is a member. You may find that your normal broker will be strongly against your wishes to trade in derivatives, in which case you may need to get a second specialist broker for you LIFFE deals. To make a deal, you call your broker who then telephones an assistant on the floor of the exchange. The assistant gives your order to a trader in the pit, who yells and signals until he gets you a deal. The paperwork is processed, and then your broker calls you back to tell you that your order has been executed.

Options

An 'option' is simply an option to buy or sell shares, other financial instruments or commodities at a pre-agreed price within or at a certain time. LIFFE deals with options on shares, share indices and interest rate futures.

Let's consider some of their characteristics:

- they have no 'real' value
- they don't give you voting rights in a company
- they have a limited life and are worthless once they have expired

Traditional options have existed for centuries, but have become far less popular following the recent introduction of traded options, which are examined in the next section.

Traditional options:

- have a life of three months
- must be exercised at the end of the period (but not before) or allowed to expire

In the past, options were used by experienced professionals to hedge and speculate, often in quite an informal way. Since the 1970s, they have been developed to make it easier for outsiders to trade in them – hence the term 'traded options'.

Traded options

The form of traded options is fixed by the options market, which sets the rules. The reason for this is that in order to make them easy to trade, options must be standardised. Equity options (options on shares) are available on LIFFE for about 70 large companies. You can find the price information on options in many national newspapers. The big difference between traded options and the traditional ones is that you can buy and sell a traded option as often as you like during its life. As well as the market in shares, you can also buy traded options based on the FTSE-100 share index.

Like any game, you have to learn the rules and the jargon before you can play. Here are the basics.

Puts

A 'put' option gives you the right to sell shares. You pay a small percentage of their price for the option.

EXAMPLE

Wayne is 18 and has just discovered traded options. He thinks that Megabucks plc's shares are going to drop within three months. He buys a put for 28p per share on 1,000 Megabucks shares – their market price is currently 284p. Wayne has laid out £280 for his option and watches Megabucks' share price avidly.

After ten weeks of ups and downs in the share price, it finally drops to 250p. Wayne's guess has been right. He quickly exercises his option by 'putting' it on to an option dealer – this means that he claims his right to force the dealer to buy his shares. Wayne doesn't own any Megabucks shares, but he can now buy them at the lower price, or he could if he had the cash, which he doesn't. Fortunately, he doesn't have to come up with the money because his broker can make both transactions almost simultaneously and simply send him his profit, which is:

Income from sale of shares at 284p		£2,840
Less:		
Cost of option	£280	
Cost of shares at 250p	£2,500	
Profit		£340

Lucky Wayne! He has made £340, less dealing costs, in ten weeks on an outlay of £280. If his guess had been wrong, he would have only lost the £280.

Calls

A 'call' option gives you the right to buy shares. As with puts, you must pay a small premium for the option.

EXAMPLE

Flushed with success on his previous gamble, Wayne is ready to try again. This time he thinks that Lotsadough plc's shares are going to go up within three months from their current price of 284p. He is quoted 28p per share for a three-month call, and decides to take the risk, buying the call on 1,000 Lotsadough shares. His outlay is £280.

Once again, Wayne gets it right. Within the three months, Lotsadough's shares go up to 350p, and he exercises the option, forcing the dealer to sell him 1000 shares at the old price of 284p. His broker sends him a cheque for the profit, which works out as:

Option cost	£280	
Shares bought at 284p	£2,840	
Shares sold at 350p		£3,500
Profit (before dealing costs)		£380

The psychological appeal of options

You can see what's going to happen next. Wayne is going to go on and on trading in options because it is such easy money – all you have to do is guess correctly. You tell yourself that all you stand to lose is the cost of the option. Then you start increasing the number of options you are buying. Then, if you are unlucky, once you have bought thousands of pounds' worth of options, a big market hiccup occurs for reasons you couldn't possibly have anticipated (it's always so unfair!) and all your options expire, worthless – let's hope you haven't spent all your profits on buying more options, or worse still, borrowed money to buy them. What Wayne should do if he enjoys the game is try to get a job as a trader – he'll probably make much more money that way, and he'll get all the trading excitement he wants as well.

Speculation in options seems to be particularly appealing to people with a good head for figures; to them, there is something utterly absorbing and pleasurable about the incessant abstract calculation of probabilities.

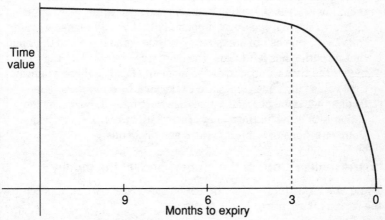

Figure 7.2 An option's time value

The premium

As we have seen, the premium is the money you pay to buy an option. Normally an option on shares costs between 8% and 15% of the current market price of the share.

The exercise price

This is simply the price at which you can exercise the option. It is also known as the 'strike' price. You will find that there will be a variety of different options available on a share with different exercise prices at any one time.

Time value and intrinsic value

Options are said to have two parts to their value – the time value and the intrinsic value. These values behave in different ways, and immensely complicated calculations are made to work out how they change over the life of an option. The premium you are asked to pay for an option is worked out by adding the time value to the intrinsic value.

- Intrinsic value refers to a positive difference between the current share price and the exercise price. For instance, if your exercise price on a put is 150p and the share is currently at 100p, the put has an intrinsic value of 50p.
- Time value is harder to grasp. It is the amount by which the premium exceeds the option's current intrinsic value, and measures the mathematical probability that you will make a profit from the option before it expires. The time value relates to the time that an option has left to run; the more time there is left, the higher the time value, and at the moment of expiry there will be no time value left. Time values are worked out by computers. The factors that influence time values are the time left, how near the option is to being 'in the money', the volatility of the underlying share or commodity, interest rates and dividends.

'In the money', 'out of the money' and 'at the money'

These are terms to describe the option's exercise price in relation to the current share price:

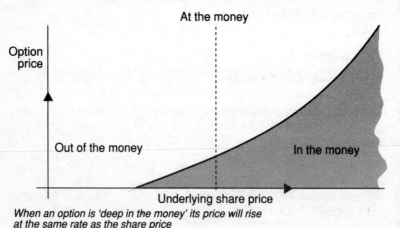

When an option is 'deep in the money' its price will rise at the same rate as the share price

Figure 7.3 How option prices relate to share prices

- 'in the money' is where the option has intrinsic value
- 'at the money' is where the exercise price is approximately equal to the share price
- 'out of the money' is where the exercise price has no intrinsic value, only time value

Hedging with options

Imagine that you own some shares which you intend to keep for many years. Reading the financial runes, you anticipate a drop in the share price in the short term. To protect yourself against the fall, you should buy a put, which should compensate you if your prediction is correct. Smaller investors have no need to hedge in this way, and will find it very costly to do so.

How to trade in options

Contact an options broker; he or she will ask you to deposit money with him, which will be used to pay for the premiums as you deal. When you instruct the broker to deal, the broker will try to get the price you ask for. As with share dealing, options brokers offer different types of service, such as execution only, advisory and discretionary services, each with a different scale of commissions.

Why do investors buy traded options?

Private investors are attracted by the 'gearing' possibilities of traded options, and are reassured by the possibility of limiting their potential losses.

If you buy an out of the money call and the share price goes up you will make around ten times what you would have made if you had simply bought the shares. The potential loss is the premium cost, part of which you may be able to get back by reselling the option before the expiry date.

The longer the option is, the more expensive it is because there is more chance of you making a profit. In the money options give you lower profits, but a bigger chance of making one, so they are a safer bet.

Writing options

You can 'write' an option on a share. You do this through a broker, who will look for someone to buy the option from you. The buyer pays you a premium for the option, and the broker takes a commission. If the buyer exercises a put, you must buy the shares, and if the buyer exercises a call, you must sell the shares. You can write options on shares you don't own. This is called 'naked writing', and, if you don't have the funds to back up the risk, it is a very dangerous activity.

A real-life example

In another book, I wrote in a similar vein about options, and received a number of letters from a reader, Peter Hicks, who enjoys writing options. Here are some extracts from his letters:

EXAMPLE

. . . I have found writing naked puts to be most rewarding: a way of making money without actually holding stocks and using up the annual tax-free capital gains allowance of around £12,000 for a married couple whilst leaving one's capital safely on deposit.

'In April (1996), I fancied Lucas. My hunch was reinforced by [an analyst's newsletter]. I toyed with the idea of buying 4,000 at about 213p – but I would much prefer to buy 4,000 at 200p! So, I 'put' myself at risk to **have** to buy 4,000 Lucas at 200p at any time up to November. For taking this so-called risk (I would be quite happy at 200p) I received a cheque for £420, net of all expenses – a nice tax-free bonus to add to the interest on my uninvested capital. I will only have to purchase the stock if the price falls below 200p but will only lose if the price falls below 189½ whereas if I had bought the stock at 213 I would have lost £940.

At present (September 1996), Lucas has enjoyed a spurt to over 230 and if the price continues rising you will say I have lost by selling puts instead of buying the stock or call options but I am more than happy with my limited gain of £420 in advance, taxfree. In November, when the options expire worthless I can look around for another hunch and write some more puts . . .'

. . . An interesting point in the traded options market is that buyers far outweigh sellers. Many institutions are forbidden to be sellers by the terms of their constitutions. Loosely, there are too many punters (buyers) and too few bookies (sellers). Hence, traded options tend to be a sellers market and prices favour sellers, I believe – particularly put sellers . . .

. . . We are completely in accord concerning writing uncovered 'calls'. That said, you will note that one of my May expiries is a naked Redland 460 call position! In fact, I hold Redland through my PEP (not on margin). I could afford to see Redland go through the roof and still smile, being content with the limited profit at 460p. The dodgiest May expiry was BTR – the market price was getting ever closer to 300 as expiry approached and, in fact, dropped below 300 the day after expiry – a very near miss!

Sold Contract Note

Name of broker

We have sold for
client ref. no.

Name of client   Option expires   16.10
Trade option account   20 Nov. 96

Bargain date and tax point   For cash settlement
15 Apr 1996

Time dealt and quantity	Stock name	Price	Bargain conditions	Amount
Ex time 11.02	4 LUCAS INDUSTRIES	11.5p		£460.00
OPENING BARGAIN	PUT OPTIONS NOV 96 / 200			

Commission minimum vat exe	£30.00	
VAT exempt	£ 0.00	
Other expenses	£10.00	£ 40.00
	Total	£420.00

Figure 7.4 A sample contract note for traded options

Mr Hicks is an experienced private investor of many years' standing and has funds outside the market to back up his speculation. It is inadvisable for an inexperienced investor to follow his methods. Please note that neither the author nor the publishers are rendering investment advice in reproducing the above extracts, which are given for information purposes only. If you are interested in getting into traded options, you should seek professional advice.

Warrants

A warrant is a kind of long-term option to buy shares at a certain price. Moguls and executives involved in the mergers and acquisitions of companies sometimes have warrants as part of their remuneration packages – for instance, a director may be given warrants to encourage him or her to get the company to perform better.

The main difference between options and warrants is that when you exercise a warrant it usually means that the company issues new shares, thus diluting the share capital.

Some companies issue warrants to their shareholders to encourage investment. For instance, for some years BTR has given warrants free to its existing shareholders, with an exercise price which is just out of the money.

In general, warrants are only suitable for wealthy investors, and even they should only really have 5% or so of their portfolio in warrants.

Summary

Here is the main point you should know about derivatives.

- Small investors should avoid them. If you absolutely must dabble in derivatives, earmark a sum of money, which you can easily afford to lose, for the purpose. Mentally kiss the money good-bye, seek advice and training, and then start trading.

8

FOREIGN CURRENCIES

Although the heady complexities of exchange rates and the currency policies of nations seem far removed from the needs of smaller investors, it is worthwhile to learn something about them, since they have direct effects on the UK economy and on your own financial freedoms. In this chapter we will look at:

- Why do nations have their own currencies?
- The Bretton Woods system 1945–1972
- Exchange controls
- What is an exchange rate?
- The floating rate system
- The black hole
- The foreign exchange (forex) market
- Can you predict exchange rates?
- How exchange rate changes affect investments
- Currency funds
- A single European currency

Why do nations have their own currencies?

The right of an independent nation to mint its own currency is well established, and states tend to guard this right jealously. The reason is quite simple – control of the nation's currency is one of the chief ways that a state steers its own economy. Economically speaking, nations are in competition with each other in the same way that different businesses compete; if a country allows its economy to be dominated by other nations, it tends to become poorer.

As the world gets smaller, however, the economies of different countries become increasingly interdependent, so a degree of international co-operation is necessary. The alternative is economic and political isolationism; Albania, for instance, became so isolationist after World War II that its only strong economic ties were with China. This policy did nothing for the prosperity of the country and Albania is now the poorest, least developed country in Europe. With examples like this before them, governments generally realise that it is sensible to co-operate with one another – the question is not whether we should co-operate, but how much. The agonies over monetary union in the EU illustrate how difficult it is for countries to work in close partnership with one another.

The Bretton Woods system 1945–1972

In the aftermath of World War II it was obvious that some kind of new international monetary system was needed. With many countries in ruins – in 1945 the main currency in use in Germany was cigarettes – something had to be done to stabilise the chaos and rebuild what had been destroyed in the war.

Before the war ended, the Allied nations held a conference at Bretton Woods in the USA to agree on a plan. They founded the International Monetary Fund (IMF) and the World Bank, and set up an international monetary system which was supposed to give stability to exchange rates. This system came to be known as the 'Bretton Woods system'.

At the end of World War II it was plain that the USA had become by far the most economically powerful country in the world, and was holding around two-thirds of the entire world's gold reserves in Fort Knox. It was natural, therefore, that the US dollar should be chosen as the benchmark currency against which all other currencies were measured. The US agreed that the dollar could be changed for gold at

$33 an ounce – this gave some reassurance to foreign governments, businesses and private investors that any dollars they got hold of were worth more than just the paper they were printed on.

All other currencies were defined in terms of dollars, at a published, fixed rate of exchange. At the time, fixed rates were vital – how could anyone export or import in the ruins of Europe or Japan if they didn't know what their money was going to be worth next week? It was agreed that if a country wanted to change its rate of exchange against the dollar, it had to make a formal announcement that it was going to do so. That way, businesses could adapt to the change without going to the wall. In 1949, 28 countries devalued their currencies against the dollar.

As people began to rebuild their countries and become prosperous again, world trade mushroomed. Powerful corporations amassed vast funds of money which they could switch from one continent to another very rapidly without the permission of governments, and the Bretton Woods system was gradually undermined.

By 1971, the US decided that the Bretton Woods system was hurting its own interests. Without obtaining the agreement of other countries, it announced that it would no longer exchange gold for dollars and, at the same time, devalued the dollar against other currencies. The system had done its job – 25 years after the war, the world had returned to prosperity.

Exchange controls

One of the features of the post-war period was exchange controls. Exchange controls are imposed by governments to prevent the free movement of money in and out of their countries. In the UK, for instance, for many years the exchange controls were so restrictive that you could only take a few pounds with you if you went abroad – not enough even for a holiday. Exchange controls are bad news for the private investor, since they restrict your freedom to invest your money where you want, and to take it somewhere else when you want to do so. More recently, South Africans have suffered greatly from this problem; they have had great difficulty in exporting money from their country.

——— What is an exchange rate? ———

An exchange rate is the ratio at which you can exchange one currency for another. If you can get three deutschemarks for one pound sterling, the ratio is £1:DM3, or you could express it as DM1:£0.333. Usually there is a convention about which way round the ratio is given for any particular two currencies.

If the exchange rate changed from £1:DM3 to £1:DM4, you could buy more deutschemarks for your pound. The pound has become 'stronger' against the mark, and the mark has become 'weaker' against the pound. Another way of saying exactly the same thing is to say that the pound has 'appreciated' against the mark, and that the mark has 'depreciated' against the pound.

All this is straightforward, but you can get confused if it is not clear which way round the exchange rate is being expressed. If someone is saying that a certain exchange rate has risen, always double check to see which of the two currencies now buys more of the other.

Hard and soft currencies

These are loose terms to describe the volatility of a particular currency – most people would call the deutschemark a 'hard' currency in the 1990s, because it has tended to get stronger against other currencies and Germany has low inflation. In the 1920s, however, the mark was a 'soft' currency during the period of hyperinflation under the Weimar Republic. Most currencies in the world are generally thought to be 'soft'.

——— The floating rate system ———

After the Bretton Woods system collapsed, there was no longer any 'benchmark' currency. Although much international trade is still done in dollars, the 'greenback' had lost its all-powerful status. This was a reflection of the new realities, where countries such as Germany and Japan had developed extremely powerful economies and their currencies had consequently become more desirable.

Since the 1970s there has been no formal, fixed link between the world's currencies, and no currency is guaranteed by gold. The rate at which you can change one currency for another is now simply the 'going rate', which is changing constantly. This arrangement is described as the 'floating rate' system, because the relative values of currencies are 'floating' up and down against one another according to the economic 'weather'.

Floating rates have had their advantages. For example, during the oil crises of the 1970s, when oil-producing countries attempted to take a harsh line against the oil-consuming countries, the flexibility of floating exchange rates helped to reduce the confusion – the currencies of the oil producers, such as Saudi Arabia, suddenly became much more valuable, which is why there was a sudden influx of high-spending Arab sheikhs into the fleshpots of London and New York. A few years before, they could barely afford to go abroad – now they could take over floors of the Ritz and the Dorchester, and hand out £100 tips to taxi drivers. This was a direct result of a change in the exchange rate between the riyal and Western currencies.

EXAMPLE

John is a gift shop owner who has cash savings of £10,000. He has earmarked £1,000 of it for a foreign holiday with his girlfriend Sue. They want to go to Azania, an exotic African country. They've been planning the trip for months, and have learned a good deal about the prices and facilities available in Azania. Suddenly, a dramatic macroeconomic event occurs which means that £1 buys 10 times more Azanian crowns than it did before. When John and Sue arrive in Azania they find that they can live like lords on a few pounds a day. John quickly has £5,000 transferred from his savings account to Azania, and embarks on a spending spree on high-quality local art – he gets tremendous value on his purchases, which he takes home to sell in his shop.

The disadvantages of floating rates

If exchange rates had still been fixed during the oil crises of the 1970s, the Western economies would have ground to a halt, temporarily at least. This does not mean, however, that the floating rate system has no problems. The main ones are as follows.

- Floating rates are highly volatile. This means that there is a much greater need for hedging in currencies by means of derivatives (see Chapter 7).
- Individual nations are tempted to try to manipulate the exchange rates of their own currencies. This only works for a few years at most, but it creates confusion – as well as opportunities – amongst international investors.

The way that a country manipulates its exchange rates is by using its central bank – in the UK, this is the Bank of England – to act like a huge dealer in the foreign exchange markets. The bank buys or sells massive amounts of its own currency to try to force the exchange rates in the direction it wants them to go. This is financed ultimately by borrowing and taxation.

EXAMPLE

Suppose that a UK government decided that it wanted to make the pound 20% weaker against the currencies of the countries to which it exports the most goods. A weaker pound would have the effect of making the sterling price of UK goods seem cheaper to foreign buyers – they can buy more goods for the same amount of money.

All other things being equal, the foreign buyers should pile in and buy more UK goods, in the same way that John bought more art in Azania in the previous example. This would be good for the UK companies that sell them those goods and, hopefully, for everyone else in the UK too, because more money will be coming into the country from abroad and it will 'trickle down' through the system.

In order to make the pound weaker, the Bank of England starts selling lots of pounds in the international currency markets – principally the buyers will be banks and dealers. This has the effect of flooding the currency market with pounds, so its 'price' (which is its exchange rate) will be less than before.

All things are not equal, since governments, banks, companies and dealers across the world will notice what the Bank of England is doing and respond to it. Numerous other factors,

---

too complicated to explain in this book, will come into play, and ultimately the Bank of England will have no more pounds to sell, unless it borrows more or prints more, either of which causes inflation, and this may be against government policy, as it is at present.

The black hole

It is often said that if you get three economists together you will get five different points of view. Economics is not an exact science, and there is a sense in which there are no right answers to the world's financial problems, despite pompous people's assertions to the contrary. Perhaps the solution is a kind of Utopia where poverty and inequality are genuinely and permanently abolished, but until that happens – and in my opinion it never will happen – we can be fairly sure that economic crises will occur from time to time.

There is an anomaly that shows why nobody ever knows exactly what is going on; it is called 'the black hole' in the balance of payments.

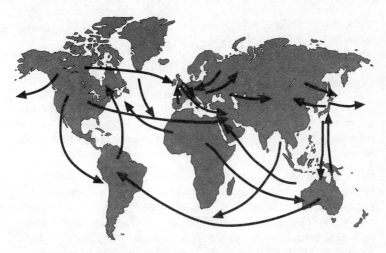

Money flows around the world all the time, but if you reconcile the balance of payments of all nations, they don't add up. This suggests that balance of payments figures are not accurate; is someone cooking the books?

Figure 8.1 The black hole

The balance of payments of a country is like the annual accounts of a company. It shows the country's debts and assets, the money that it has spent abroad and the money it has received from abroad during the year.

If you collect the published annual balance of payments figures for all the countries in the world and reconcile them, they ought to all add up. It's a bit like a card game – if at any time during the game you stopped everything and counted all the cards, there should always be fifty two. The trouble is that the balances can't be reconciled – each year they are out by many billions (the 'black hole'). This means that some of the accounts must be wrong, in the same way that if you stopped a card game and there were 50 cards instead of 52, you would know that something was wrong.

The existence of the black hole is a good joke on those politicians and economic commentators who try to pretend that balance of payments figures give cast-iron, reliable data from which unquestionable conclusions can be drawn. The truth is that no-one, not even governments, has a completely accurate picture of the world's economy. It is important to realise this if you are an investor because it helps to explain why so much economic commentary and information is contradictory.

The foreign exchange (forex) market

The forex market is arguably the only really global market in the financial world. As we have seen, governments try to influence it, but since the emergence of the floating rate system it is not under anybody's total control.

Forex dealing is done all over the world, but the main centres are in London, New York, Tokyo, Zurich and Frankfurt. The big dealers are banks, brokers, companies and large investors who buy and sell currencies from most of the world's countries. It's a frantic world where exchange rates change rapidly and unpredictably. Hundreds of billions of pounds' worth of currencies are bought and sold every day.

The dealing is done for five main reasons.

1 Normal banking – people and companies go to a bank to buy, say, dollars with pounds, so the bank has to buy in dollars for 'stock'.
2 Hedging – as we saw in Chapter 7, banks need to hedge against many different variables in the course of their business, and may buy foreign currencies, or currency futures, to do so. Any company that does business overseas may hedge against possible changes in an exchange rate by buying a currency future (it's actually known as a 'forward rate'), just as a commodity producer will buy or sell a futures contract in his product.
3 Arbitrage – this means buying something and selling it instantly at a profit. In the forex market, most arbitrage is done by special departments in banks which use highly sophisticated equipment to search the world for arbitrage opportunities. These opportunities often only last for minutes. Arbitrage has the effect of keeping the quoted exchange rates in different financial centres around the world in line with each other.
4 Speculation – this means guessing that particular currencies will strengthen or weaken against others, and then putting your money where your mouth is. Since politics can affect exchange rates, some guesses are made on the basis of political, as well as economic, analysis. A famous example of speculative success is when the fund manager George Soros allegedly made a profit of about £100 million in forex deals when the UK dropped out of the ERM in September 1992 – the so-called 'Black Monday'.
5 Central bank action – this was discussed on page 104. Central banks buy and sell in the market principally to influence the position of their own country's currency, or to attack that of another country.

– Can you predict exchange rates? –

In the short term, exchange rates are highly volatile and unpredictable. Many businesspeople and investors, however, have an instinct about how medium- to long-term exchange rates may affect their plans. In the world of finance this is known as 'taking a view', but it can simply be a gut feeling. Consider this example.

EXAMPLE

Mike is a television scriptwriter. He is offered the equivalent of £40,000 to write a script for a German company. The money will come in stages over 18 months, although the actual work involved will only take about four months in total. He decides to accept the offer because this is a good chance to save a nice chunk of capital – should he ask to be paid in marks or pounds? He decides to take the fees in marks – he can keep them in a bank account in the Channel Islands, and either invest them or change them into sterling for spending in the UK. By keeping the money in marks until the last moment, he reckons he might make some extra money because he instinctively feels that the mark is going to get stronger against the pound over the next few years. He realises that if he is wrong he might lose a little money on the exchange.

Mike is no economist and he doesn't follow the forex market. He doesn't even read the papers every day. It is simply that he travels a lot in Europe and he has 'taken a view' about the medium-term pound/mark exchange rate. He thinks the pound is a bit soft.

The following year Mike is offered a similar deal by a Turkish film company. He doesn't have to think twice to know that he doesn't want to be paid in Turkish liras – he'll take dollars, marks or pounds. This is because the lira is a soft currency, and Mike is afraid that it might depreciate against the pound quite quickly.

How exchange rate changes affect investments

In Chapter 9 it is argued that investors who invest some of their assets outside the UK benefit both from diversification and a chance of better returns. If you want to bring this money back into the UK, however, you are running a risk that exchange rates will go against you at the wrong moment. Broadly, here is how exchange rate movements affect foreign bonds, shares and cash.

- Bonds – if a country's interest rates fall, the value of its bonds will generally rise. Countries with strong currencies generally offer lower interest rates on their bonds to countries with weak currencies. For smaller investors, investing in foreign bonds is not usually worthwhile because in order to get better interest rates than you can at home you will have to take the risk that exchange rates will go against you, and the bonds themselves will usually be less safe than gilts, on which the UK government has never defaulted.
- Shares – if you own shares in a company that is quoted on one of the volatile foreign stock markets, you may well get an extraordinarily good return. Even if exchange rates go against you, the extra profit may well be worthwhile.

EXAMPLE

Sally buys £100,000 worth of shares in a company quoted on the stock exchange of one of the 'emerging market' countries – let's call the country Narnia and its currency doubloons. When she invests, the pound/doubloon rate is 1:2. A year later, her investment has performed well – it has shown an increase of 50% and Narnia's inflation rate has remained low. Sally decides to sell her shares because she thinks that Narnia's economic bubble is about to burst. She checks the exchange rate, which has changed to £1 to 2.5 doubloons, and then does her sums.

Amount invested was	£100,000
This bought shares valued at	200,000 doubloons
Selling the shares will get her	300,000 doubloons
Converting this to sterling at 1:2.5 £120,000	

For the sake of simplicity we will ignore dealing costs, inflation and exchange costs. Sally sees that because sterling has strengthened against the doubloon, her return will not actually be 50%, but only 20%. Even so, this is still a decent return, and since she doesn't want to risk staying in the Narnia market, she sells the shares and brings the money back to the UK.

- Cash – if you hold foreign currencies, their sterling value will be changing constantly. Much depends on what you intend to do with the cash. If it is simply being used as a temporary home for money that will be put back into UK shares later, then it might be safer to keep it in sterling unless you 'take a view' that the currencies are going to strengthen. If you need to hold foreign cash because you intend to spend it abroad, you can either hold it in the currency of the country where you intend to spend it, or in hard currency which you can convert when you need to.

Currency funds

As we have seen, a great deal of speculation goes on in the forex markets, and investors can participate through specialist funds which deal in currencies. These funds are generally based in tax havens, and some may not be well regulated. For the smaller investor, the returns you are likely to get will not be good over the long term, particularly since there will be management charges to pay, as with all collective investments.

A single European currency

We live in interesting times; the European Union is the major political issue affecting the UK, and a huge controversy rages about how far the UK should go in surrendering its sovereignty to EU control. From an economic point of view, the problem is essentially to do with the massive structural changes going on in the world's economy. An economically united Europe could become a virtual super-power, or at least prevent individual European countries from becoming impoverished as the world's manufacturing shifts to the Far East. On the other hand, there are fears that a centralisation of power in the EU could damage democracy. These fears are not restricted to the UK alone – many other Europeans have painful memories of previous attempts at centralisation, such as those of Hitler and Napoleon.

Federalists (those in favour of greater centralisation) want to create a single European currency. 'Monetary union', as it is called, would make it much easier for the EU to act as a single force on the stage of world business. One currency would mean one basic interest rate across the EU and no chance of currency devaluations by member states. Trade between member states would be greatly simplified, and might well become more efficient.

The essential problem of bringing about monetary union is getting all the member states to agree on the details. Countries like Portugal, Greece and Ireland are poor, and need financial help from the richer countries if they are to be fully integrated on equal terms. Germany is the richest country in the EU, and has been prepared to pay a substantial proportion of the costs, but the unification of the two Germanies has been extremely expensive, and the prosperous West Germans have been feeling the pinch. Meanwhile, France's generous social welfare system is becoming increasingly expensive to operate.

No-one can be sure that monetary union will come about. At the time of writing (summer of 1996), the grand vision of a single currency seems to be fading, but no-one knows what will happen. Investors have to live with this uncertainty.

Conclusion

The floating rate system and abolition of exchange controls have broadened the field of opportunity for private investors. There is no reason to suppose the it will last for ever. A world monetary system has been proposed which would be intended to limit the degree to which currencies could move against each other. Such a system might well create artificial distortions in values, and draconian exchange controls could follow.

Taking a long-term view, investors might do well to keep some of their assets abroad – outside the EU – to protect themselves against the introduction of new restrictions. In the next chapter we will examine ways of doing this.

9
INVESTING ABROAD

Investing abroad is important for diversification, but introduces added risk and costs. In this chapter we will look at:

- Why invest abroad?
- The world's stock markets
- Direct investment
- Pooled investments
- Tax havens
- Opportunities for expatriates
- Banking offshore

Why invest abroad?

As the financial press never tires of telling us, we are now in an era of global financial markets. Every week we read stories of brash traders making fortunes in faraway places and dire warnings of the imminent demise of Western influence in the face of the growing industrial power of the 'Pacific Rim' nations. Then there are the mysterious 'emerging markets', in which canny investors are said to make fortunes overnight. Can all of this be true, and if so, should you be investing part of your money overseas?

As we saw in Chapter 8, the world is currently going through a period of freedom from exchange controls. Let's hope this will last – it is definitely good news for the private investor, since you are free to move your money in and out of the UK as you wish. This freedom also has a lot to do with the excitement in the world's financial markets. Many countries, some of them tiny and under-developed, are now committed to allowing foreign investment through their stock markets. The trouble is that not all stock markets are the same; liquidity, costs and regulations vary from market to market, and some are alarmingly volatile. As we will see, this causes serious problems for the unwary.

The reality is that basic investment principles apply whatever country or company you choose to invest in. The main arguments for investing overseas are as follows.

- Diversification – just as you wouldn't normally hold just one company's share in your portfolio, it makes sense not to keep all your investments solely in the UK.
- Better returns – it is perfectly plain that some other countries are going to grow much more vigorously over the coming decades than the UK will. A relatively small investment in a foreign company could mushroom dramatically in a few years. The hard part is, of course, picking the right company to invest in.

The main arguments against investing abroad are as follows.

- We should be backing Britain by keeping our money at home. Personally, I disagree – Britain has always been a trading nation, and people who make fortunes abroad may well spend them at home, as they have done in the past.
- It's too risky. This is a more convincing argument. There are certainly many foreign investments which should be left to the professionals. There are, however, increasing opportunities for the smaller investor to participate in other countries' prosperity at acceptable risk levels.
- You'll lose a fortune if exchange rates move against you. This danger is greatest when you are dealing with 'soft' currencies and countries with economies that are out of control.

What kinds of overseas investments should you consider?

The first thing to do is to decide how much of your money you should place overseas. A good rule of thumb is not to put more than 25% of your 'risk investments' abroad; that is, not more than 25% of your total available assets, not counting your home, pension fund, insurance policies and rainy day money.

Next, you must decide how to spread the investments across cash deposits, bonds, shares and pooled investments. You can apply the same rules as were outlined on page 11.

In the case of cash deposits and bonds, some investors are attracted to very high interest rates which are offered in foreign countries from time to time. Usually this is too risky – either the high rates don't last for long (sometimes only a few days) or you lose out by a fall in the value of the foreign currency. This is essentially a game of currency speculation which can be safely left to professionals. Pooled investments which specialise in foreign bonds and currencies are also to be regarded with caution. It may make sense, though, to hold some hard currency offshore as rainy day money, especially if you own a home abroad or take many foreign holidays.

This leaves direct investment in shares, or investing in shares through unit trusts or investment trusts. You are still taking some currency risk, since sterling may strengthen, so you need to be reasonably confident that the returns will be good enough to cancel out any currency losses. Before looking at this in more detail, we should first examine some of the foreign markets.

—— # The world's stock markets ——

There are over 60 different stock markets in the world, ranging from the New York Stock Exchange, which is the biggest, to the tiny exchange in Croatia, which offers only a handful of shares. Here is a whirlwind tour of some of them.

- The New York Stock Exchange (NYSE)
  The NYSE is one of three New York stock exchanges and is the biggest. Like other US exchanges, it is well regulated by the Securities and Exchange Commission (SEC). The main index is the Dow Jones Industrial Average (DJIA), which gives the arithmetic mean average of share price movements of 30 important companies listed on the NYSE.

- National Association of Securities Dealers Automated Quotations
  (NASDAQ)
  NASDAQ was started in 1971, and is very high-tech. It works as
  an international system of trading in shares and bonds via
  computer screens. It was the first foreign exchange to be recognised
  by the DTI in the UK.

- The Tokyo Stock Exchange (TSE)
  This is the biggest of eight Japanese exchanges. The main
  Japanese index is the Nikkei Stock Average, which is price-weighted
  and includes over 200 Japanese companies. Many people had their
  fingers badly burned when the market crashed a few years ago,
  and there have been many scandals relating to improper practices
  such as 'ramping', which means pushing shares at small investors
  for the benefit of insiders. The best way into this market is
  probably through a unit trust or an investment trust.

- The Stock Exchange of Hong Kong (SEHK)
  The SEHK boomed in the 1970s, and had a major crash in 1987. It
  is a very important market internationally, but it remains to be
  seen what will happen once China takes Hong Kong back from the
  UK in 1997. The main index is the Hang Seng.

- European exchanges
  Traditionally, people in continental Europe have preferred bonds to
  shares, and stock exchanges are looked on with suspicion there.
  France and Germany have the biggest markets, with Frankfurt
  being the largest centre. In Germany only banks can act as brokers,
  and shares are issued in bearer form, meaning that they are
  registered anonymously.

- The 'Tigers'
  These are Japan, Hong Kong, Taiwan, Singapore and South Korea.
  Apart from Tokyo and Hong Kong, Singapore is the most open to
  foreign investors.

- The 'Dragons'
  These are Thailand, the Philippines, Malaysia and Indonesia.
  Their populations save a large proportion of their incomes, which is
  a sign that their economies are soundly based. The Dragons are

fast becoming heavily industrialised societies, and will probably be the world's main manufacturing base in the future.

- The primary producers
  These are Australia, New Zealand, Canada and South Africa.
  They are well developed and modern, but make their money from exporting raw materials and commodities. This makes their markets quite volatile.

- The emerging markets
  This is a catch-all term to describe stock exchanges which have just started up, or have been given a new lease of life, in developing countries. They include countries such as Mexico, Brazil, India and Turkey. Some have done very well, while others have not – they are all certainly very volatile.

───── Direct investment ─────

The main problems with investing in foreign markets are practical ones.

- Dealing costs vary widely. Bid offer spreads may be very wide for transactions under £10,000 or so.
- You are too far away to act quickly, especially in volatile markets.
- There may be a language problem.
- How do you find a broker you really trust?
- Some markets are not well regulated and there is a real danger of fraud.
- The cleverest, most knowledgeable brokers are to be found on the biggest of the world's exchanges, not on the smallest ones.
- Illiquidity can be a major problem – what's the point in having made a huge profit if you can't sell your shares?
- The currency risk.
- Differences in regulations and terms can catch you out; for example, you may suffer unexpected penalties if you do not settle on time.
- Every country has its own tax rules, and you need to make sure that you will not lose out by being taxed twice, once in that country and again in the UK.

- It is difficult to interpret the news if you do not live locally.
- Many foreign shares are denominated in large amounts –
  hundreds, rather than in pennies or pounds.

If these caveats have not put you off direct investment, then you can either deal through a London broker or contact one in the market you want. Going direct to a foreign broker should be cheaper, but make sure he or she is governed by 'best advice' rules. An important point to consider is that, overall, UK companies earn nearly 50% of their profits from business overseas anyway – so you can get some of the benefits of foreign growth by investing in some large UK companies.

Pooled investments

There are some excellent unit trusts and investment trusts that have done well in foreign countries. You can find some of them listed on the London Stock Exchange, while others may be based offshore and listed elsewhere. There are also index funds, which follow one of the indices of the major markets, such as Tokyo and New York. If you are a small investor, pooled investments are probably the only realistic way to invest abroad, and they are also the most simple.

Remember, though, that even if you are investing in sterling the fund itself will still be subject to currency risks.

Tax havens

The expression 'tax haven' is not very precise – it covers a whole range of no tax and low tax states and territories which specialise in many different types of financial services. Multinationals, companies and private individuals are all catered for. Tax havens come in all shapes and sizes, and may be strictly regulated and highly respectable or pirate dens full of fraudsters and cut-throats! For the private investor who hopes to stay within the law, the following tax havens are the most suitable:

- Bermuda
- The Channel Islands
- The Dutch Antilles
- Liechtenstein
- Monaco
- Switzerland

This is not to say that other tax havens should never be used, but simply that the ones listed above are wealthy, well governed and are on reasonably good terms with the rest of the world. This is good news for the private investor, because you need to be able to take money out of a tax haven as well as to put it in, and you need to feel reasonably sure that the banks and professionals in the havens are properly regulated and honest.

If you think that tax havens are immoral and should not exist, remember that the older ones were used to save many people's lives and assets when they had to flee the Nazis in the 1930s, and that, even today, tax havens often provide the only chance of escape for refugees from oppressive regimes all over the world.

Uses of tax havens

UK residents are perfectly entitled to hold assets overseas but, as long as they are resident in the UK, they must pay taxes on those assets. The main point to bear in mind here is that if you work abroad for more than a year, you may be able to avoid UK income tax and capital gains tax (CGT) during that period, so once you return to the UK those assets will remain untaxed if they are kept in certain tax havens and not brought into the UK. The section on expatriates on page 123 gives more details.

It is vital to get professional advice before making any arrangements to put money into a tax haven, since the Inland Revenue has many complex rules on how such money may be treated for tax purposes.

Here are the main ways in which private investors use tax havens.

- As a place to make bank deposits. The Channel Islands, for example, do not tax interest on bank deposits, and while you may be liable to UK tax on the interest, you will be paying it in arrears, so the return will generally be better.
- As a place from which to speculate in foreign currencies. Banks in the better tax havens usually offer good facilities for switching currencies rapidly and cheaply.
- As a place for a holding company or trust which owns assets in

another country. If, for example, you have a holiday home in Europe, you may be able to mitigate taxes by forming a company in a tax haven which legally owns the property.

● As a place from which to trade in the global stock markets, or simply to hold shares in pooled investment funds such as investment trusts.
● As a place to hold assets in preparation for permanent emigration or retirement to the tax haven or another country.

None of these uses is a wildly exciting, get-rich-quick scheme, but they do have the advantage of being legal while circumventing many tedious restrictions that burden residents of the UK and other 'onshore' countries.

Retiring to a tax haven

A general rule of thumb is that the better the tax haven is, the richer you have to be to emigrate to it. Jersey, Monaco and Switzerland, for example, do everything they can to discourage everyone but the very rich from settling. The reason for this is obvious – like most countries, these havens want immigrants who will make their country richer, not poorer. If you want to retire to a tax haven, but cannot meet the entry requirements of the top-notch havens, here are some countries which may be suitable.

● The Bahamas (and many other Caribbean islands)
● Cyprus
● Malta

In these countries you will usually pay no tax, or less tax than you do in the UK. The main thing to remember once you have retired is that you will avoid UK tax only if you make short, infrequent visits to the UK and if you don't have 'accommodation available for your use' (a complex Inland Revenue definition) in the UK once you have left.

Offshore trusts

A trust is a legal concept invented and developed by English lawyers over many hundreds of years, and is now recognised by many countries all over the world. Trusts are 'resident' in a particular country, so although UK trusts have few advantages for tax avoidance, offshore trusts offer much more freedom of choice. There are very many uses for a trust – the main ones are:

- safeguarding collectively owned funds, such as pension funds
- protecting life assurance policy holders and their dependants
- building up a group of international businesses
- saving tax
- passing money on to beneficiaries while protecting it from others

Trusts can be expensive to maintain, especially if they are offshore. You probably need at least £100,000 to put into an offshore trust before it becomes economic to do so.

What is a trust?

A trust is created by a legal document called a 'trust deed' or 'trust instrument'. It can't own anything itself; the trust's assets are owned by the trustees of the trust, who cannot use them for their own benefit. A trustee can be a private individual or a company, and has heavy legal obligations to manage the trust's assets properly. For this reason, trustees are usually paid for the work they do.

The person putting the money into a trust is called the 'settlor'. The people who will eventually receive money from the trust are called the 'beneficiaries'. A settlor can also be a beneficiary, as is the case when you contribute, as a settlor, money to a pension fund and later you draw a pension from the fund as a beneficiary.

Perhaps the easiest way to understand trusts is to think of them as gifts in slow motion, passing from the settlor through the hands of the trustees to the beneficiaries.

Aren't offshore trusts only for very rich people?

The short answer is yes – but it depends on your own definition of 'rich'. As people grow older and find themselves with increasingly complex responsibilities, trusts can offer a solution to some of their problems, assuming that they have at least £100,000 that could be put into a trust. As we will see in Chapter 13, even UK trusts can be used to mitigate inheritance tax, but this is only one reason why you might consider using one – more commonly, trusts are used to protect beneficiaries from themselves and others. To see why, consider the following example.

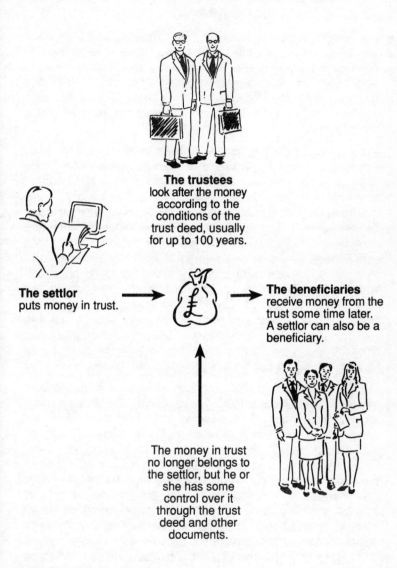

The trustees look after the money according to the conditions of the trust deed, usually for up to 100 years.

The settlor puts money in trust.

The beneficiaries receive money from the trust some time later. A settlor can also be a beneficiary.

The money in trust no longer belongs to the settlor, but he or she has some control over it through the trust deed and other documents.

Figure 9.2 How a trust works

EXAMPLE

Tim and Vanessa are married and in their fifties. They have both been married before to foreigners, have several children by different marriages and Tim has also had a child out of wedlock. About ten years ago their business activities really took off, and they have become wealthy people. Their main plan now is to reduce their work load and ease themselves gently into retirement.

The only cloud on the horizon is their children's future. Both Tim and Vanessa agree that they want to reduce inheritance taxes as far as possible, but they do not want to pass control over large sums of money to any of their children until they are mature enough to handle it. In the case of two of their children, Tim wonders if they will ever be mature enough to handle money – although they are in their thirties, they are spoilt and it doesn't look as if they will ever settle down to a job. Another child has a serious drug problem, and a fourth is physically handicapped. Two other children are sober and sensible, but their father, Vanessa's vindictive ex-husband, has an unhealthy influence over one of them. Vanessa and Tim want to do their best for all the children, but agree that each has different needs, and are worried that various ex-spouses and hangers-on will try to grab money if they get the chance.

They decide to set up offshore trusts with their children as beneficiaries, in each case making special rules and arrangements for how each child will receive the money. In the case of the handicapped child, for example, their main goal is to make sure that there will always be enough money to pay for his care, and that no unscrupulous carer can misuse the funds. In the case of the two spoilt children, they stipulate that the funds can provide them an income for life, but that no capital can ever be passed on to them. All these arrangements take a lot of time, thought and expense, since there are many legal points that must be considered, as well as possible political and legal changes in the UK, in the tax haven where the trusts are based, and in the countries where some of their children are domiciled. There's no rush, though; after three years of mulling it over in great detail, Tim and Vanessa set up the trusts and monitor them carefully ever after.

── Opportunities for expatriates ──

If you ever have the opportunity of working in a low-tax country for a few years, don't dismiss it out of hand – it could be the biggest chance of rapidly accumulating capital that you ever get. This happens when you are paid a higher salary abroad than you receive at home, and suffer little or no tax in your country of employment. In such cases, you can avoid paying UK taxes by investing in offshore funds based in tax havens. As long as this money is not brought into the UK, it accumulates tax free.

EXAMPLE

Rachel takes a job on a three-year contract working in one of the Gulf states; she is paid £6,000 a month, which is more than double what she earns at home and, what's more, it is tax free. Even though life is dull and expensive, Rachel manages to save £4,000 a month. She puts it in respectable investment trusts based in a tax haven and, by the time she returns to the UK, she has a fund worth over £200,000. Since she already has a home and savings in the UK, she leaves the fund to grow offshore, tax free. If she eventually decides to retire abroad her offshore fund will generously supplement her retirement income, and if she decides to bring it back to the UK at some time in the future she will still have had the benefit of some tax-free growth.

What companies offer

Not all expatriates prosper; much depends on your employer and on the country in which you are working. At best, life as an expatriate gives you:

- lower or no income tax
- a higher salary
- free or subsidised housing
- an income from letting your home in the UK
- school fees, transport and health insurance paid by your employer

- extra allowances such as the 'foreign service premium" (FSP) and the 'cost of living allowance', which can be saved rather than spent

The main advantage that the expatriate has is the chance to save money quickly. It is usually harder to trade in the stock markets if you are working abroad, so expats need to invest conservatively.

A warning

It is important to be wary of financial advisers who work overseas; they mingle with the expatriate communities and will generally approach anyone who has recently arrived from the UK. No doubt some of them are good at their jobs, but many of them are not properly regulated. Here are some warning signs that an overseas adviser may not be safe.

- You are asked to invest in obscure, loosely regulated stock markets.
- You are told that you will get extremely high returns at no risk.
- You are invited to put money into a very complicated scheme which you don't understand and which you will not be able to control.
- You are invited to break the law in some way.

The best way to arrange your affairs as an expatriate is to continue to use the professional advisers you already have in the UK. They can help you regularise your tax affairs and put you in touch with good offshore advisers if necessary.

Banking offshore

'Banking offshore' simply means banking in a tax haven – most of them are islands off the shores of large continents. As we have already seen, there is nothing illegal about having an offshore bank account as long as you declare it to the Revenue and pay any tax due. The main reason to have an offshore account is to transfer money easily between other countries and currencies.

EXAMPLE

Jane has an Italian holiday home, but finds it convenient to pay large domestic bills in Italy from an account in Guernsey. This is because she doesn't like keeping cash in Italy – a few years ago she had an account there, and woke up one morning to find that a substantial sum had been taken from it by the government as part of an emergency measure to cope with one of Italy's frequent economic crises. 'A holiday home is more of a luxury than an investment,' says Jane, 'but why should I put up with daylight robbery if I don't have to?'

Opening an account

It is fairly simple to open an account in a tax haven; here's how.

1 Go to a central public library where there are telephone or business directories of the tax havens you are interested in. Make a list of the banks' names and addresses. If you can't visit a public library that has these, telephone one of the big reference libraries for help.
2 Write a letter to each of the banks you are interested in, keeping it short and to the point. Tell them how much money you will be depositing initially, and give them some idea how much will be going through the account. This is necessary because some banks will not accept small accounts. Ask for information about the bank, such as its annual report.
3 Write to the Chamber of Commerce, Finance Ministry or similar authority in each tax haven and ask them to send you general information, and also if there are state guarantee schemes in the case of a bank's failure. You will find the addresses in the same telephone books as the banks.
4 As the replies start to come in, you will find it quite easy to weed out a lot of candidates, either because they don't want your business, or because they do not offer the services you need.
5 Once you have made a shortlist, compare their details carefully. Charges and facilities will vary, as will the size and ownership of the bank.

6 If you have the time, go and visit the banks on your shortlist. Write to them first and arrange an appointment.

7 Don't be concerned if the banks want to know a lot about you. There is currently a great fear of money laundering, and banks in the better tax havens, such as the Channel Islands, are under a lot of pressure to 'know their customers'. It is in your interests to be above board, since banks have been known to freeze suspect accounts.

8 It is probably not a good idea to keep more than 15% of your assets in any one bank, in case of disaster.

9 If you can't visit the bank, you can go through the whole procedure by letter if necessary.

10 When you open an account, the bank will ask for information from you, including specimen signatures, and references from a bank or building society in the UK.

All this may sound like hard work, but it is in your interests to take the trouble to shop around before choosing a bank – after all, you may be entering into a relationship with it that lasts for decades.

Summary

Here are the main points covered in this chapter.

- Many foreign economies are likely to perform better than the UK's in the coming years. It makes sense to invest a part of your assets overseas in order to improve your returns.

- Overseas stock markets vary widely in their dealing costs, business terms, regulation and tax regimes. Illiquidity can be a big problem in some markets.

- Foreign equities offer a better chance of beating adverse currency movements than do cash deposits or bonds.

- One way of getting into foreign investments is by buying the shares of multinationals quoted in London.

- Smaller investors are better off using unit trusts or investment trusts than investing directly when investing overseas. This should reduce both risks and costs. Direct investment is often possible, but there are logistical and administrative problems in dealing with foreign brokers.

- The better quality tax havens offer expert advice and sophisticated services for the international investor.

- When planning how to pass on money to your dependents, consider using an offshore trust if you are relatively wealthy.

- If you work abroad in a low-tax country, save as much of your income as you can to accumulate a nest egg. This money can be kept offshore, and you will save some UK tax. Check with your financial adviser on how to regularise this arrangement with the Inland Revenue.

- Offshore banking is useful if you are moving money across borders. Take the trouble to shop around before choosing a bank.

10

PROPERTY

In this chapter we will look at:

- Owning your own home
- Financial characteristics of property investment
- Types of property
- Land law
- Mortgages
- Using your equity

Owning your own home

In Chapter 2 we saw that owning your own home is usually an important part of your overall saving strategy. This has not always been the case – as little as 70 years ago, the prosperous middle classes preferred to rent their homes rather than to own them. The reasons for the change are complex, but for the individual, it boils down to the question, 'would my money be better off in property?' In the 1920s, the answer was 'Yes', and at present it is 'No'.

Here are the main arguments in favour of owning your own property.

- Since World War II, UK property has generally been a good inflation hedge, and many individuals have made large capital gains by selling their own homes.
- There is no CGT on capital gains from selling your own home.

Good tax planning can enable a family to avoid CGT even if they own, between them, several properties.

- Cheap borrowing – for almost everyone, raising money by mortgaging a building is the cheapest form of borrowing.
- Mortgage repayment costs can be equivalent to the cost of renting. This is true, but not all the time, nor in every location.
- Borrowing to buy a home forces you to save – for many people, repaying the mortgage is their only financial discipline.
- People who own their own homes generally treat them better than people who rent them – even if you are hopelessly impractical, you will inevitably become interested in such weighty matters as loft insulation and the best way to repair plaster.

Financial characteristics of property investment

Every home owner thinks he or she is an expert on the residential property market, and more nonsense is talked about it than almost any other type of investment. Here we will look at the essential characteristics of property investment which apply to all types of buildings, be they residential, commercial or industrial:

- an imperfect market
- illiquidity
- high maintenance costs
- high transaction costs
- expropriation
- legislation against property owners

An imperfect market

There is no single 'property market'; values of similar properties vary by region, and the distance of a few miles, or in some cases a few hundred yards, can make a huge difference to the values of two otherwise identical buildings. Although there are indices published which purport to give an indication of general price movements, they don't tell you about the price of a particular building.

It is difficult to discover purchase prices and rents obtained from particular properties, so even experienced valuers find it hard to assess the exact market value of a building.

In practice, all this means that the property markets are 'imperfect' – in other words, that it is possible to purchase bargains at all times if you have superior knowledge. Contrast this with the stock market, where the abundance of skilled players make the market 'efficient' and bargains hard to obtain (see page 62).

Illiquidity

This brings us to another important characteristic of all properties; it takes time to sell them, and it is hard to predict how much you will get for them. This means that you have to make sure that you have other, more easily saleable assets as well so that you can raise cash quickly if necessary. Property owners can get squeezed if property taxes, interest rates or maintenance costs go up.

High maintenance costs

Unlike many financial securities, which can be stored for years without attending to them, all properties need regular maintenance. Neglected properties lose value and can become dangerous, which, incidentally, makes them bargains for experienced renovators. It is sometimes hard to estimate the amount of maintenance costs in future years, particularly the cost of major repairs.

High transaction costs

Whenever you buy or sell a property, you will probably incur the following costs:

- solicitor's fees
- estate agent's commission (when selling)
- stamp duty (when buying)
- mortgage arrangement fees
- moving expenses
- looking expenses

Any kind of investment will incur some dealing costs, but they are particularly high for properties – perhaps 5% if you sell a house for £100,000. In other countries dealing costs can be even higher. There are many ways to reduce transaction costs, however. If you are willing to do the legal paperwork yourself, you can save on solicitor's fees – read *The Conveyancing Fraud* by Michael Joseph (see Bibliography) for more information about this. Likewise, it is possible to negotiate low estate agency commission, or avoid it altogether if you sell privately. Other costs can be reduced too, particularly if you shop around when you are raising a mortgage.

Expropriation

Property is vulnerable to expropriation during wars, economic crises and political upheavals. Buildings are conspicuous and immovable; it is very easy for a government to take them away from their owners, either directly or through taxation. In the UK we enjoy a degree of security of property rights that many other countries lack – but in every century certain classes of property owners are forced into selling, and it is not always the rich who suffer. In the 18th century, for instance, smallholders had to sell their land for cash as part of a land reform known as the 'enclosures'. Unless you see this kind of trend coming, there is little you can do. If you are alert, you should be able to divest yourself of your properties in good time.

Legislation against property owners

Rich countries like the UK seem to have a love–hate relationship with private property ownership. On the one hand, they want everyone to benefit from the joys of owning their own homes, while on the other they want to limit profits, particularly those of landlords and developers, and to protect the rights of tenants.

Most countries have 'rent control' legislation to protect tenants. This creates a separate market in rent-controlled properties, which will have a lower value than equivalent unencumbered properties. In the UK some tenants are able to rent properties permanently at miniscule rents, while others have to pay well over the odds with virtually no security of tenure. If rent controls become too harsh, property values drop and the market becomes sluggish. Despite the difficulties, if you have a working knowledge of the law and you choose your properties carefully, you should still be able to profit from your investments.

If you invest in a foreign country, make sure that you study the rules very carefully. It is not unknown for a government to offer attractive concessions to foreign property investors, only to impose punitive taxes once enough people have been persuaded to buy. Not long ago this happened in Spain, when property-related taxes in Marbella and elsewhere rose by 2,000% in one year.

Ten other features

Here are ten other characteristics of property as an investment.

1 The 'unit cost' of a property is high. This means that large holdings can only be had by the very wealthy, be they individuals, companies or financial institutions.
2 If you manage a property as a landlord, whether for private tenants or for companies, you can greatly improve its value by judicious refurbishment and re-development.
3 Property is traded in a variety of ways, including auctions, estate agency and private advertising. This allows the experienced investor to 'buy low and sell high' by timing his movements while switching between markets.
4 Property is heavily regulated by the state. Restrictions on tenancy, construction and usage can increase the risk of a property investment.
5 Some buildings, particularly commercial and industrial properties, 'wear out' after only a few years. The value of the land may not be affected.
6 You can hold different kinds of title to a property. These include:

   – freeholds, where you own the land and possibly the building which stands on it,
   – long leaseholds, which can be as long as 999 years, and
   – short leaseholds, which are called 'wasting assets' because their value decreases to nothing as the lease expiry date approaches.

Different types of title have different tax implications; for example, pension funds avoid paying tax on rental income, which can make short-term leases more attractive to them than they are to taxpayers.

7 Some properties are less risky than others. Prime properties, which are those properties which are thought to be of the best investment quality, are the most liquid and thus the least risky.

8 Rents can be volatile and, in the case of commercial and industrial properties, tend to rise only at intervals of five years or more at the time of rent review. Although rents tend to rise in monetary terms, they may not increase in real terms, and there is also the risk that there may be periods when you cannot find a tenant.

9 Unlike the stock market, it is not easy to get reliable information on market activity. The property industry has been known to feed the press misleading information from time to time.

10 Property is cyclical. During a slump or stagnation property owners must sit tight until things improve. In booms, lots of people make money, and prices soar; inevitably, there comes a time when prices cannot go higher, and start to fall. Surviving as a property investor depends largely on being able to pay the interest on money you have borrowed, even when interest rates have risen and property values have fallen.

Many home buyers are not very sophisticated; they pay the market price for a property even when the income you could get if you rented it would be far lower than the cost of the mortgage. Many people will say that any gains you make when you sell a property will be cancelled out because you must always pay an equivalently high price for any house that you move to. This fails to take market cycles into account.

To understand the consumer mentality in property, consider the UK property crash of 1989: in the preceding few years almost everyone saw huge gains in the value of their properties, far outstripping inflation. Thousands of young people thought that they would never be able to buy a home if they didn't buy immediately. It seemed as if prices would continue to rise for ever, and many estate agents, solicitors and money lenders busily encouraged this view. Mortgage borrowing was easy, and people even exaggerated their incomes in order to borrow more. When interest rates rose and the crash came, homeowners at the bottom of the property ladder were the worst hit. People had paid upwards of £65,000 for poorly built dwellings in the grimmest parts of London in 1988; six years later these properties were going for around £25,000 at auction. Lenders began to repossess homes where the borrowers could not service their loans, and sold them quickly at prices which were lower than the outstanding mortgage. This meant that some people who had lost their homes found that they still owed some of the money that they had borrowed.

Since 1990, the government and financial institutions have worked to reduce the problems in the market, and at the time of writing (1996), property prices look as if they have stabilised.

Types of property

The main categories of interest to private investors are:

- undeveloped land
- residential property
- commercial property

Undeveloped land

Undeveloped land tends to keep its value – they aren't making any more of it! It is illiquid and doesn't produce much of an income, but you can be fairly confident of holding it for the long term as an inflation hedge. If you want to improve its value, you can try to get planning permission for development; over the years, opportunities to succeed at doing this may arise as the local authority planning needs change. If you buy a field a mile or so out of a growing urban area, you might make a fortune as it grows out to meet your land. Choose land in an area you know well, and make sure you have it properly surveyed; you don't want to discover that there is radioactive waste underneath it later! In general, don't try to develop the land yourself – getting the planning permission is where most of the money is made.

Residential property

Your main residence is exempt of Capital Gains Tax, so you can keep all the profit you make when you sell it. This is the main engine that powers the movement up the property ladder; people who can afford it tend to move into a series of increasingly more valuable properties over the years, making tax-free gains each time they do so. This strategy has worked for several decades, but may not continue to do so in the future. An added advantage is that you can get mortgage interest relief at source (MIRAS) on the first £30,000 of your mortgage, which reduces your borrowing costs (see page 137). While married couples are only allowed CGT exemption on a single home, unmarried couples are allowed to have a home each.

If you want to become a residential landlord, the situation becomes more complex. Currently, landlords are afforded reasonably good protection if they let properties using an Assured Shorthold Tenancy for a minimum of six months; this allows reasonably easy eviction of tenants at the end of the term or in case of default, but you must follow the rules strictly, especially on such matters as the timing of the service of notices to the tenant. If you do not, there is a danger that you will get a sitting tenant who cannot be forced to leave, which reduces the value of your property. A residential landlord is actively running a business, with increased risk and possibly increased rewards. For more on active investment in general, see Chapter 12.

Commercial property

The law on business tenants is more friendly to landlords, so some investors buy shops and offices to let out. Although the risk of getting a sitting tenant is much lower, the risk of losing rent because of default or bankruptcy may be higher, especially in the case of smaller traders who take on premises and then find that their business fails. Once again, this kind of investment is essentially an active business with a relatively high degree of risk.

Property bonds and time share

These are essentially packaged investments designed for consumers rather than investors.

- A property bond is a scheme linked to insurance which gives you holiday accommodation based on a points system.
- Time share is where you buy the right to use a property for a certain period each year, in perpetuity. Usually there will be annual charges as well as a capital sum to pay.

Neither of these schemes is likely to offer as good a return as if you were to invest directly in a property, although some time shares may be worthwhile.

Investing through quoted property companies

There are a number of property companies in the stock market, and you can buy their shares. If you do so, you should apply the same criteria as you would when buying any other share and, in addition, you should study the characteristics of this industrial sector – remember that property companies are likely to have high gearing and that the valuation of their assets may be uncertain.

Becoming a developer

Property developers are not very popular with the public; they are in a tough business, so if you want to become one, make sure that you are not faint-hearted! Amateurs should stay away from developing, except for very small schemes such as straight-forward renovations of houses, flat conversions and building extensions.

Land law

Land law is exquisitely complicated, and you will need the services of a specialist lawyer if you become actively involved in property. There are many anomalies to do with the tenure of property which offer business opportunities to the specialist investor who has sufficient funds to pursue them. If you are attracted to this, it is a good idea to get a grounding in land law, perhaps by training as a 'Licenced Conveyancer' (see Useful Addresses), so that you can cope with some of the intricacies on your own.

Mortgages

Most property investment relies on borrowing, so it tends to be a high-geared activity. In this section we will examine some of the main features of raising and using mortgages for your first home. While this is technically 'consumer' borrowing, the basic principles hold true even if you are borrowing to purchase investment property, the main difference being that lenders will look at your past experience as a landlord and the potential for rental income, rather than exclusively at your own income from employment.

Mortgage interest relief at source (MIRAS)

If you are raising a mortgage on your main residence, the Inland Revenue allows you to claim tax relief on the interest payment on the first £30,000 of the loan. The relief has been reduced in recent years and is currently 15% (from April 1995); it is almost always deducted from the gross mortgage repayments made to the lender, so that you only pay the net interest each month, on the first £30,000 of your mortgage. The lender gets the rest back from the Inland Revenue.

EXAMPLE

Lucy has a loan of £40,000; this month her gross repayment is £400. How much will she pay after tax relief?

Only the first £30,000 is eligible, so she gets relief on £300 of her total repayment of £400: 15% of £300 = £45.

Her net repayment this month will be £355.

How much can you borrow?

There are various types of mortgage available, but before examining these, you should try to get a grasp of why there is a limit, peculiar to you, on how much you can borrow. Unless you are rich, you can't just go and borrow £5 million to buy a luxury mansion, because the lender wants to be sure that you can pay the money back over the period you have borrowed it for. It is important to get this limit right, because, among other things, it dictates the price you are able to pay for a property. If you are a first-time buyer, you will probably buy somewhere fairly cheap to begin with, with the intention of buying a bigger place later when you are earning more money. The process of progressively selling one home to buy a more expensive one is called the 'property ladder'.

The amount you can borrow depends on the five main factors shown in Figure 10.1.

1 Your income	Lenders will advance a maximum sum based on a multiple of your income
2 Your liabilities	as long as you haven't already got too many debits.
3 Your deposit	Lenders like to see you investing some cash too
4 Your credit history	and that you pay your bills
5 Your employment status	and that you are unlikely to become unemployed.

Figure 10.1 Lending criteria for private home buyers

Your income

Most lenders are happy to talk about the amount they are willing to lend you (which can vary a lot between different lenders) well in advance. The amount they will lend is usually calculated by using 'income multipliers'.

You may hear phrases like 'three plus one' and 'two-and-a-half times joint'. 'Three plus one' simply means that the lender will lend a couple three times the higher income plus one times the lower income where a couple is buying a house jointly. 'Two-and-a-half times joint' means 2.5 times the total income of a couple.

A single person can borrow less than a couple because there is only one income to use for the repayments.

EXAMPLE

Suppose Carol and Rob are buying a house together. Carol earns £20,000 and Rob earns £9,000. How much can they borrow?

Using a three-plus-one multiplier the maximum loan available will be:

```
        3 × £20,000 =    £60,000
plus 1 ×   £9,000 =    £9,000
Total maximum loan =   £69,000
```

Using two-and-a-half times joint multiplier:

2.5 × (£20,000 + £9,000) = £72,500

Total maximum loan = £72,500

Suppose, however, that Carol earns £15,000 and Rob earns £14,000. Their total joint income is the same as before (£29,000), so on the two-and-a-half times joint multiplier, their maximum loan would be the same as before, but using the three plus one multiplier:

```
        3 × £15,000 =    £45,000
plus 1 × £14,000 =    £14,000
Total maximum loan  =   £59,000
```

The maximum loan available will be £59,000, £10,000 less than before.

This is one reason why it pays to shop around the different lenders to find out who will lend you the most.

How much of your income will the lender allow in the calculation?

Your income may come in many ways, including:

- your salary
- your guaranteed overtime
- your overtime which is not guaranteed
- commissions
- unearned income (e.g. from investments)
- guaranteed bonuses
- unguaranteed bonuses
- part-time income

Each lender decides which of these parts of your total income can be taken into account when deciding how much to lend you.

In general, if your income is guaranteed or you can prove that you have received it regularly over, say, the last three years, the lender allows the full amount of income to be included in the multiplier. If some part of your income is not guaranteed, the lender will either not allow it at all, or only allow a proportion of it to be taken into account.

Proof of your income

Most lenders want proof that you earn what you say you do. This can take the form of the last six months salary slips, P60s for the last two years, or an income reference, which is a questionnaire sent to your employer which asks for the details of your income and for confirmation that your job is permanent. The form requires a company stamp and the signature of someone in authority in the company.

If you are self-employed, you are usually asked to produce three years of audited accounts to prove your income. This is used for the income multiplier. If you do not have three years of audited accounts, sometimes a letter from your accountant will do – this varies between lenders.

The lender looks for as much security as possible in order to stop you from overstating your income and borrowing more than you can repay.

Why do people try to borrow too much?

It was not only in the housing boom that people tried to borrow too much – it happens all the time. One of the main reasons why people do it is that they are in a rush to buy their dream house, which always seems to be a little bit more than they can really afford.

It is in your best interests, as well as the lender's, not to borrow more than you can afford. It is not impossible to fiddle your income statements in various ways to make it look as if you earn more than you do. My advice is – **don't!** Not only is this fraud, and you could be taken to court for doing it at a later date, but also it is foolish because you will have terrible trouble making the repayments if you have borrowed too much. Lenders hate repossessing houses almost as much as you would hate to have your house repossessed, so respect their experience in this matter.

Your liabilities

All lenders have to make sure that you can afford to repay the monthly instalments without being financially overstretched. As mentioned above, if you take on too high a commitment you are in danger of not having enough money to make the repayments, especially if interest rates increase, which will push up the monthly repayments.

To avoid this, the lender looks at what else you have already borrowed, including:

- amounts on credit cards
- HP agreements
- bank overdrafts
- mortgages on other properties
- tax bills owed by self-employed people

EXAMPLE

Suppose that Jane and Jim are a couple wanting to buy a house. Jane's salary is £14,000 and Jim's is £10,000. They have an HP loan for £2,900 which costs £69 a month for the next four years and owe £500 to a credit card company. They say that they pay off the credit card balance every month.

Supposing that the lender uses the three-plus-one multiplier, it may take these steps.

---

1 Calculate the maximum loan in the normal way.

3 × £14,000 = £42,000
1 × £10,000 = £10,000
Total   = £52,000

2 Subtract the HP loan from the total.
£52,000 − £2,900 = £49,100

3 The lender will probably ignore the credit card loan, and offer Jane and Jim £49,100.

There are other ways of accounting for your liabilities, so this is yet another reason to shop around.

The amount of your deposit

When house prices were rising in the 1980s, many lenders were happy to lend 100% of the value of the property because they thought that the value of the property would increase, covering the debt and giving the borrower a profit. Since then, property prices have been falling, which has made lenders stop lending 100% mortgages. At present you will be unlikely to be able to borrow more than 90% or 95% of the value of the property.

The difference between the amount you owe on your mortgage and the price you would get if you sold your house is called the 'equity'. If you are, say, a second-time buyer with some equity, you will be able to borrow, but it has caused trouble for many first-time buyers who do not have a deposit.

The main benefits of having a deposit are:

- your monthly repayments will be less
- the cost of insuring against not being able to repay the loan will be less
- you will have a wider choice of lenders and may be able to get better terms

Your credit history

Lenders also check your creditworthiness. Creditworthiness used to have a sort of pseudo-moral aura around it – if you had never been badly in debt, you were somehow a better person than if you had been. This ethos still survives, but these days people are more realistic, and know that anyone can make a mistake.

What lenders want to make sure of, though, is that you are not the kind of person who never stops making 'mistakes' about their money. They may do this in several ways.

- They may interview you. The main reason for the interview is to probe into whether you are trying to borrow too much. People who work in the lending industry are not known for having rich imaginations, so try not to worry them by saying or doing anything that they might think is odd.
- They may ask for a reference from your existing mortgage lender, if you have one, to see that you were good at making the repayments.
- They may ask for a reference from your landlord to see that you pay the rent on time.
- They will check to see if you are a bankrupt, or have been, and whether you have any county court judgements (CCJs) against your for debts.

If these checks throw up something the lender doesn't like, you may be refused a loan, or only get it after a lot of explaining.

Your employment status

Lenders don't like lending to people who have job hopped over the years and have no real 'track record' – they prefer people who can show a steady career development with one or two employers over a number of years. This is a bit old fashioned, considering that many of us change jobs these days through no fault of our own, so if you can present a good case you should be all right.

Lenders prefer to lend to people whose skills are always likely to be in demand in the labour market, for example skilled carpenters, doctors, and graphic artists. If you are, say, an actor or a rock singer, the lender may be doubtful about your ability to remain in work. The lender wants you to have a steady employment record and to seem 'stable'.

Types of mortgage repayments

The most common types are shown in Figure 10.2.

Mortgage type	You pay
Capital and interest (repayment)	Interest and capital – mainly interest in the early years
Endowment policy	Interest to lender Insurance premiums against a sum to repay capital
Pension contract	Interest to lender Pension contributions – much of the pension will pay off capital loan
PEP	Interest to lender Contributions to investments held through a PEP – the PEP fund will be used to repay the capital

Capital and interest (repayment) mortgages

Until the 1980s this was the most popular way of repaying a mortgage. As the borrower, you were given a regular (usually monthly) repayment to the lender over an agreed period of time (typically 25 years). This method is regaining popularity at the expense of endowment mortgages, which were popular in the 1980s and are now increasingly being seen as expensive.

With repayment mortgages, part of each repayment is used to pay the interest on the loan, and the rest is used to repay part of the amount you borrowed.

In the early years of a repayment mortgage, the largest part of the repayment goes to pay the interest, so the loan itself is paid off very slowly indeed. For example, after ten years of a 25-year repayment mortgage it is unlikely that you will have repaid much more than 10% of the original loan. In the later years, more and more of each repayment goes to repay the outstanding capital, and the amount of interest payable reduces.

Life assurance policies with capital and interest mortgages

Most lenders insist, or at least strongly advise, you get life cover so that a mortgage may be repaid when you die. This protects the interests of anyone you leave behind if you die as well as the interests of the lender. As the outstanding amount you have borrowed reduces each year, you progressively need less insurance to repay it, so the most appropriate life policy is a 'decreasing term assurance policy'. Although the premiums remain the same throughout, the level of death benefit reduces each year, roughly in line with the expected reduction in the loan.

Endowment mortgages

With endowment mortgages you only pay the lender the interest on the loan, but make no regular payment to reduce the outstanding loan itself. Thus the amount you initially borrowed should neither increase nor decrease during the mortgage term.

In order to repay the loan, you take out an endowment policy to repay the loan at the end of the agreed period. You pay the premiums, and when the policy matures, the loan is repaid, but this depends on the investment performance of the policy.

There are many types of endowment policy; they are all types of 'whole of life' insurance. There is no doubt that they were 'oversold' during the 1980s.

What you should **never** do, particularly in the early years, is to surrender the policy, because the surrender value will be very low or non-existent. With endowment mortgages this would be a serious problem, because you are relying on the value of the policy to pay off the mortgage.

A 1989 National Consumer Council survey found that 25% of people with endowment mortgages had cashed in their policies and taken out new ones when they moved house, when they could have simply 'topped-up' their existing policy, avoiding the problem of poor surrender values. They were poorly advised.

- Keep your endowment policy until the end of its term – don't cash it in early.
- A low-cost endowment policy assumes a certain level of annual growth necessary to repay the loan at the end of the mortgage term; if the rate of growth is not achieved then the cash at maturity will not be enough to repay the loan fully.
- Mortgages based on a full (with or without profits) endowment policy do not guarantee that the original capital will be repaid.

Pension mortgages

These operate in a very similar way to endowment mortgages in that you only pay the interest on the loan to the lender, and make no repayment of the capital. The capital is eventually repaid from a pension policy. A pension mortgage is the most expensive type of mortgage in terms of what you repay monthly, in spite of the favourable tax treatment that pensions get, but it will pay you a residual pension after you have paid back the mortgage.

It is often not enough to take out a pension contract to produce a fund only just sufficient to repay the mortgage; with personal pensions, for example, only 25% of the eventual fund may be taken as a tax-free lump sum, which means that a fund four times bigger than the mortgage must be achieved if the loan is to be repaid in full, when the pension benefits are taken.

The Inland Revenue requires that pension policies should be taken out primarily as a way of saving for retirement; they should not be sold primarily as a way of repaying a mortgage.

PEP mortgages

These have become increasingly popular; they are based on the principle of making regular interest-only payments, and repaying the mortgage loan from a separate fund such as a PEP or a unit trust or investment trust savings scheme. PEP mortgages are the cheapest kind of interest-only mortgage, but they are the most risky, because they are tied closely to the stock market. To reduce the risk, lenders tend to want the PEP fund to be invested in unit trusts rather than directly in shares.

Interest options

There is quite a variety of interest options to choose from.

- Fixed rate mortgages – these give you certainty about your monthly repayments for an agreed period (usually five years) by fixing the interest you pay on the loan. There is usually an arrangement fee for this.
- Variable rate mortgages – for which you pay the 'going rate' of interest. People got caught in the late 1980s when interest rates increased quickly and thus put up their repayments unexpectedly. In the last few years, interest rates have been low.
- Low start mortgages – these are designed to help you to keep your repayments as low as possible in the first few years, and to pay more later. This is done by not demanding any repayment of the capital at first.
- Capped and collared mortgages – these are variable rate mortgages with fixed upper and lower limits of interest, which gives you a degree of certainty about the cost of your repayments.
- Deferred interest mortgages – these are the opposite of low start mortgages. In the early years you pay back capital but not the interest. For this to work, you need to be fairly sure that you are going to be earning more in the future and that the value of the house is going to go up.
- Discounted mortgage – this is simply a discount on the variable interest rate for a certain period. It is usually designed to attract first-time buyers.

A lot of people try to be too clever about the interest payments; the main point to remember is that you will have to pay interest, and whatever scheme you choose there will probably be times when you are paying more than someone else with a different scheme.

Which type of mortgage should you have?

Repayment mortgages are safe, boring and back in fashion. Other mortgages are a bit more exciting, because they hold out a promise of extra benefits. When the economy is booming, the prospect of actually getting these benefits seems realistic. When the economy is contracting, people have trouble making their monthly payments, and things look dark. This is all part of the cyclical nature of all economies (not just the UK's). Lenders understand all this perfectly well – it is every-one else who gets confused. Whichever mortgage you decide to have, your primary objective should be to make sure that you are going to be able to pay it back without having a desperate struggle. This means not borrowing too much, and being realistic about your future income – it may also mean living in a smaller place than you would like for a few years.

Using your equity

'Equity' is the difference between the value of your house and how much you have borrowed. It is the part of the value of the house that belongs to you. If you did not have a mortgage, you would have 100% equity in your house.

It can be very tempting if you are a home owner to borrow money against the equity in your home. People often find themselves in a position where they have equity in a house, but no cash. Here are some common reasons why people borrow against their equity:

- starting a business
- paying off debts
- pay for school fees
- go on holiday

Suppose you own a home worth £100,000 and a mortgage of £60,000; you therefore have equity of £40,000. Perhaps this represents more money than you have ever actually had in cash at any one time in your life. Why shouldn't you spend some of that money? It's yours, isn't it?

Here are a few arguments for and against doing so.

- Any loan you raise in this way will be secured against your house – this means that it is relatively easy for the lender to cause your house to be repossessed if you miss repayments. Lenders of this kind of loan are generally less tolerant than the lender of your main mortgage.
- Consider how you are going to use the money; couldn't you save up for the thing you want?
- In times of high inflation, it may make good sense to borrow against equity if its proportion is high, because it may improve your return.

Getting a further advance from the existing lender

Probably the most convenient way of releasing equity from one's home – and often the cheapest way – is for you to apply to your existing lender for a further advance. The existing loan will remain intact, and if the lender agrees to the loan this new advance may be effected over the remaining term of the initial loan (usually) or over some other period. There will be expenses – usually a survey of the house, and, less frequently, an arrangement fee.

Remortgages

Many lenders have quite strict guidelines on what propositions they will and will not consider for further advances – for example, quite a number will not give advances unless the money is being used for home improvements. Often the maximum total loan (including the original loan) may be restricted to a percentage of the value of the property (say 85%).

Other lenders have less restrictive lending criteria and so if you are refused a further advance from your own lender, you could seek to move your entire borrowings from your existing lender to a different source of finance. This process is called a 'remortgage' and usually consists of the new lender taking over your existing mortgage and advancing a further sum of money.

The costs involved in a remortgage are usually higher than those for a further advance. There will be:

- a valuation fee
- solicitors' fees
- an arrangement fee

These charges make this option unattractive for small further advances (say under £5,000). If you arrange a remortgage to help refinance other debts, such as credit cards and personal loans, on which you are paying high rates of interest, then it may be worthwhile in the long term.

Secured second mortgages

Most banks and building societies will try to establish that:

- you can meet the regular repayments of your loan

- you have a clean credit history (i.e. no county court judgements for bad debts)
- the security in the house will cover the loan
- the reason for borrowing further money meets their criteria (e.g. home improvements only)

Usually they carry out quite comprehensive investigations to make sure that your situation does fit their rules. Lenders in the second mortgage market usually operate to less strict rules; they provide a second loan that 'sits on top' of the main mortgage.

EXAMPLE

Your house is worth £100,000
Your mortgage is £60,000
Your equity is therefore £40,000

If you take out a second mortgage with a different lender for say £20,000, the picture will look like this:

Your house is worth £100,000
Your main mortgage is £60,000
Your second mortgage is £20,000
Your equity is therefore £20,000

If you default on your loan repayments and the lenders repossess the house and sell it, the main lender would get their money back first, and the second lender would be paid out of what was left. Suppose, for example, your house was repossessed and sold quickly for £90,000 after costs (you would have trouble preventing the lenders from doing this):

Sale of house £90,000
First lender   £60,000
Second lender £20,000
Your equity   £10,000

In this case you would get some equity back, but less than if you had had the freedom to sell the house in your own time.

Often second mortgage lenders do not want to know the reason you are borrowing the money – there are usually no arrangement, valuation or legal fees but the interest rate charged will be comparatively high. The reason why they don't want to know why you are borrowing is because they aren't going to be very patient if you default, unlike your first mortgage lender, who will generally bend over backwards to help if you are in trouble, and therefore wants to stop you borrowing unwisely.

Conclusion

Most investors will keep a proportion of their assets in property, which has generally produced a good real return since World War II. As always, no-one can be certain that this will continue to be the case, but at present the ownership of your own home still appears to be a sound investment.

The key to successful property investment, whether you are simply a home owner or you have a number of properties, is the skillful management of your borrowing – if you borrow too much, prices fall and you can't make the repayments, you may lose your properties and fall into debt, so always be cautious about how far you extend yourself.

11
COLLECTABLES

Collectables are works of art, antiques, memorabilia and similar objects. In this chapter we will look at:

- The problem with collectables
- Possible strategies
- Important markets

There is no need to include collectables in your overall investment plan; they have many drawbacks for the passive investor. If you are only concerned with getting good returns, you will not be missing much if you simply cross collectables off your list of potential investments. Nevertheless, collectables are often beautiful things which can add to your quality of life, and many people 'collect' for this reason. Other people become involved because they have inherited valuable possessions, and need to know whether to keep or to sell them.

Before looking at various types of collectables in detail, we should consider their basic investment characteristics.

—— The problem with collectables ——

The main problems with collectables are:

- illiquidity
- no income
- high maintenance costs

- the need for specialist knowledge
- the danger of rigged markets
- the danger of forgery
- unpredictable, fashion-driven markets
- underregulated markets

Illiquidity

Most collectables are 'illiquid' – in other words, it can take a long time to sell them.

EXAMPLE

Suppose you have a valuable rare book; you can take it around specialist dealers, and some of them may make cash offers. You will find that these offers are substantially lower than you might make by some other selling method. Next, you investigate auctions – and you find that the next auction for your type of book is months away. If you put it into an auction and it sells, you will probably have to wait for a few weeks to receive the proceeds. If it doesn't sell, you're back at square one. Next, you decide to seek out collectors yourself – you start hanging around book fairs and auctions, reading the specialist press and taking out small advertisements. Ultimately, perhaps, you find a buyer who will pay a good price, but it could easily take many months to do this, if not years. This is what 'illiquidity' means in practice: lots of effort and expense, low offers for a 'quick' sale, and a long time passing before you can get a fair price.

EXAMPLE

When Asil Nadir's Polly Peck plc was put into administration in 1991, the glamorous collection of antiques and paintings in its head office was auctioned off with great media hoopla. The auction was a success; less than 4% of the items were left unsold, generating £3.8 million before tax and commissions. The only people who grumbled were Polly Peck's shareholders – it is reported that the collection had cost around £7 million to

---

buy over the previous few years. During that period, Sotheby's index of English furniture prices had increased by around 70%. So why didn't the auction reflect this increase? Apart from the possibility that Mr Nadir had paid too much for the objects, the fact that everyone knew that it was a forced sale must have depressed prices; if the administrators had been able to sell off the antiques piecemeal over the years, they might have got more money for them.

No income

In most cases, a collectable does not give you any income. It just sits there, and you only make money when you sell it – that is, you only make a profit if you make a capital gain when you sell it. Meanwhile, it is probably costing you money in insurance and maintenance costs.

High maintenance costs

Valuable objects must be maintained, stored and insured. This can be expensive. They are easily stolen or damaged, and there is nothing more burdensome than having to be suspicious of tradespeople and strangers who are in your home – their admiring glances at your beautiful possessions can make you nervous.

EXAMPLE

Rosie inherits, along with her parents' house, a 200-year-old watercolour by a known painter. She takes it along to a major auction house and is told that it is worth about £2,000. Deciding to keep it for a while, she hangs it on the wall of her parents' house which she leaves empty for the winter, making sure that it is covered by the contents insurance. When she returns in the spring she is horrified to discover that a fungus has grown on the painting – the wall which it is hanging on has suffered from damp during the winter. Rushing back to the auctioneer, she is told that this damage has greatly reduced the value of the painting, but that is can be restored. She is given the name of a specialist restorer. After some legwork,

Rosie finds an expert restorer who agrees to remove the fungus for the low price of £90. When she collects the water-colour, Rosie finds that there are now blank patches on the painting where the fungus has been scraped off; she must now seek out another specialist to see if the blank patches can be repainted. This will cost more money, and she will then be faced with a moral problem – should she simply try to sell the painting as if it hasn't been restored, hoping that no-one will notice, or should she 'come clean' with prospective purchasers.

The need for specialist knowledge

You need to know a lot about the things you collect, whether they are stamps, paintings, furniture, books, fine wines or any other type of object. No-one can know everything about collectables, so you have to specialise. Serious collectors can become world authorities in very narrow fields if they collect in those fields over many years – they get to know values, the objects' characteristics, how they should be maintained and restored and where they can be sold for the highest price. You must become a connoisseur and a scholar in your chosen field. This takes a lifetime of experience and study; to win as a collector, you really need to know as much as, if not more than, the dealers and buyers.

The danger of rigged and monopoly markets

If you are not a dealer or a 'serious' collector, you are a punter. The great game of the professionals is to collude in the collection of objects when they are cheap and then to hype them in as rigorous and expensive a manner as it takes to launch a consumer product onto a mass market. This is the world of glamour, publicity, high-profile exhibitions and auctions.

EXAMPLE

The famous American tycoon, Armand Hammer, made his first great coup in Russia in the 1920s. As part of a series of complex deals, he was able to persuade the Communist authorities to allow him to import a vast collection of Tsarist art treasures, including the famous Fabergé eggs. In addition, it is alleged that he was able to obtain tools from the Fabergé workshop and employ an ex-Fabergé craftsman to manufacture extra eggs, all with the famous Fabergé hallmark.

Hammer took over large department stores in US cities, filling them with his collection. It is said that jobless Russian noblemen were paid to wander through the crowds of shoppers, making loud exclamations that they recognised certain objects as having belonged to aristocratic relatives in Russia before the revolution. During the sale, you could have picked up anything from a small object for a few dollars to an important piece for a six figure sum. While some of these purchases have proved to have been bargains, others have not; as a 'punter' without specialist knowledge, you could have had little idea of the investment potential of many of the items on offer.

The danger of forgery

Forgery is a very real problem, especially with high-value objects. Many forgers are brilliant artists in their own right who cannot get the recognition they deserve. Anything can be forged – the museums and galleries of the world are full of forgeries. The forgery business is centuries old, and there is a grey area between deliberate forgeries and reproductions. For instance, a Renaissance reproduction of a Roman bronze might be mistaken for the real thing and attract a higher price. In the Middle East, where many ancient artifacts still lie undiscovered beneath the ground, there are highly skilled craftsmen who churn out beautiful forgeries and reproductions that are difficult, if not impossible, for even an expert to identify.

In addition, there is the problem of restoration. How much can an object be 'restored' before it becomes a forgery? American buyers are known to prefer restored antiques – the high-flying US executive likes to have valuable antiques in the office, but prefers them to look 'brand new', so antiques must be repaired and repainted for that market. More sophisticated buyers will reject such restored objects.

Unpredictable, fashion-driven markets

Many Victorian painters who were fashionable during their lifetimes are no longer sought after. There are many examples of Victorian paintings which sell for less now, in real terms, than they did a century ago. Tastes are constantly changing, and every few decades there are newly rich people entering the market with their own ideas of what is worth buying. For instance, in recent years Arabs from oil-producing countries have become major collectors of Islamic art, out-bidding traditional Western collectors, and the Japanese have become major customers for European art and furniture. No particular class of object can truly be said to be safe in the long term – they are all vulnerable to the vagaries of the market.

Underregulated markets

The collectables world makes the stock market look like a nunnery. There is very little regulation and a lot of dishonesty, especially at the lower end of the business. Unless you are knowledgeable, you are a punter who, in the eyes of some dealers, deserves to be fleeced.

Possible strategies

If you can afford them, collectables can give you great pleasure. Many people enjoy having beautiful and interesting things around them, and some people get satisfaction from developing an encyclopaedic knowledge of their chosen field. If this applies to you, you may well feel that making a profit is not very important – but you will probably still want not to lose money if you sell. Here are some strategies that may help.

Buying things that are out of fashion

If you really do have taste, and are fascinated by, say, mediaeval Indian miniatures, you could buy when they are completely out of fashion, wait 50 years or so and make a killing. Of course, it may be your children who make the killing – and they'll have had to avoid inheritance taxes on your collection to do so.

American folk art, Buddhist temple paintings and African sculptures were all considered curios rather than art at one time. Now they have great value. If there is a category of attractive objects that you really like, and can buy for less than it would cost to have them specially made at the present time, then they may increase in value dramatically one day.

Bargain-hunting

You may have heard the stories of the person who recognised a hugely valuable antique at a low price in a provincial shop, or the discovery of a famous signature on an apparently worthless painting. It does happen, but you must invest a lot of effort and time in the search, so it's more like prospecting for gold than investing. If you really enjoy this kind of thing, you could make it a serious hobby, or take it up as a full-time business.

Use professional selling methods

If you build up an 'important' collection over the years, you will get to know the dealers. There may come a time when it is clear that you can liquidate your assets for a substantial profit. To get the highest prices, you must undertake a professional marketing campaign – notifying potential buyers, generating publicity for the collection, choosing the best way to sell and so on. This is what Armand Hammer, in the example on page 155, did with his Tsarist art treasures.

———— Important markets ————

Here are some points on some of the most important types of collectables.

Classic cars

Cars are exempt from capital gains tax when they are sold privately. This is because most cars depreciate each year. Classic car enthusiasts can exploit this loophole, since some classic cars do appreciate. If you make large profits, though, you will have to take care to avoid being treated as a trader by the Inland Revenue – if you don't, you could be liable for capital gains tax.

Art

It is generally accepted that the art market peaked in 1990 and then slumped. There are hopes of a recovery – but an important Picasso, sold at auction for $8.35 million in 1989, went for only $3.6 million in the spring of 1996. Overall, the value of art has dropped by about 50% since 1990. Perhaps now is the time to buy for the long term.

Furniture

Antique furniture is often very practical since you can use it to furnish your home. Much of it is cheaper to buy than a modern reproduction – a good rule of thumb when assessing how much to pay for it. Beautiful, practical pieces can be had for as little as a few hundred pounds.

Wine

Suppose you spend £10,000 on fine wine in a vintage year and store it. A few years later, it is ready to drink, and you can sell part of your purchase to recover your £10,000, and drink the rest for free. That's the theory, and in recent years it has worked for buyers of fine French clarets and vintage ports. No other wines are thought to be safe bets – even champagne, which the uninitiated might think of as an investment, isn't really safe, because it is past its best after about 20 years. The investment market in wine is basically limited to the product of about 30 chateaux in Bordeaux.

Ephemera and contemporary memorabilia

These days, even things like old postcards, cigarette cards and teddy bears can go for extraordinary prices. Pop memorabilia has been a particularly successful field, with an international appeal and rising prices for the past 15 years or so. Individual stars, however, go in and out of fashion – Michael Jackson memorabilia, for example, are said to be going for less now than they were a few years ago.

Conclusion

The usual advice given about collectables is that you should buy them because you like them, not in order to make an investment return. There are periods when their real values increase, however, and if you really do have specialist knowledge about a particular class of object you may be able to make some money.

12

INVESTING IN A BUSINESS

Running a business is essentially active investment, as opposed to most of the other investments in this book, which are called 'passive'. Active investment generally carries a far higher risk, with the potential for far higher returns. In this chapter we will look at:

- Running a business
- Entrepreneurship as a career
- Buying a franchise
- The Enterprise Investment Scheme (EIS)

Running a business

'Business' is a loose term; many employees in secure jobs in large corporations describe themselves as businesspeople. So do many self-employed people on low incomes, and so do various professionals who provide services for fees but do not take risks. The sense in which 'business' is used in this chapter is that of entrepreneurial activity – in other words, the process of getting money through trade by taking risks. Here's what a witty American Wall Street man wrote about business in the 1940s. It still holds true today:

'Most businessmen imagine that they are in business to make money, and that this is their chief reason for being in business, but more often than not they are gently kidding themselves. There are so many other things which are actually more attractive. Some of them are: to make a fine product or to render a remarkable service, to give employment, to revolutionise an industry, to make oneself famous, or at least to supply oneself with material for conversation in the evening. I have observed businessmen whose chief preoccupation was to try to prove conclusively to their competitors that they themselves were smart and that their competitors were damn fools – an effort which gives a certain amount of mental satisfaction but no money at all. I have even seen some whose chief interest lay in proving this point to their partners.

So give yourself a real good mark if you know that a business should make money, but only if you really know it.'

Fred Schwed, *Where are the Customers' Yachts?*,
Simon & Schuster, 1940

These days, there are statistics to back up a number of Schwed's ideas. Here are some examples.

- An estimate for the early 1990s suggested that almost 80% of all businesses in the UK had turnovers of £100,000 or less and the majority of these had turnovers of under £50,000. Once all the costs of running the business have been allowed for, this suggests that many small business owners will earn very modest returns for their investments and hours worked. It has to be said, though, that the 'black economy', where money circulates without tax being paid on it, is as flourishing as ever and that many small traders benefit from it.
- Another recent UK survey found that the main reason for starting a business was the desire for independence.

	%
Independence	36.0
Unemployment/insecurity	22.1
To make money	16.1
Saw a market opportunity	16.1
Inherited the business	3.6
Other/don't know	6.1

Notice that making money was the main motivation for only 16% of those who were asked.
- In a 1995 survey of small businesses in service industries, it was found that just over 60% survived the period 1990–1994. In other words, nearly half didn't survive.

- Another survey found that 20% of small businesses fail to survive the first 18 months of trading, and that over 50% close within three years.
- A self-employed business person works on average nine-and-a-half hours a day, six days a week.

Business can take various legal forms, such as the sole trader, the partnership and the limited company. There are various definitions of 'small business' based on turnover, capital and/or number of employees, and business statistics sometimes lump all the different legal forms together and sometimes differentiate between them. Nevertheless, it is plain enough that most businesses are really just a means of making a living without being employed – they are not the golden geese that some people believe them to be.

In this chapter we are examining business from the point of view of the person who 'really' knows that a business should make money, over and above a reasonable wage for the hours they put in and, in addition, over and above the return they would get if they had invested their capital in a passive investment at lower risk.

The business environment in the UK

Like many other countries, the UK is not particularly friendly towards new businesses, which flourish best in fast-expanding economies and markets. The main problems facing someone considering a 'start-up' are as follows.

- The tremendous administrative burden imposed by the authorities – VAT and employment regulations alone can crush a new business by the sheer number of hours a business-owner has to spend on paperwork. Regulations change constantly, so it is difficult to develop an efficient system for dealing with them.
- The Uniform Business Rate (UBR). More than 50% of small businesses are appealing against their UBR assessment, or are considering doing so.
- Late payment of due invoices. It is expensive and time-consuming to enforce payments through the courts. Businesses often find that they are financing much of the input VAT due from their customers – one estimate has it that on average businesses finance 30% of this VAT per quarter.

- Financing difficulties. Many businesses are financed by bank overdrafts, which can be recalled at any time. Fixed-rate, fixed-term loans are a much safer way to finance a business, but many small businesspeople find these difficult to obtain.
- Lack of know-how, particularly in the areas of marketing, accounting and the law. In a fast-expanding economy it is easier to 'wing it' than it is in our rigid, highly structured society.
- The high costs and poor value given by the professions to small businesses.

Businesses require capital

You can start up a business with no capital, but it will normally take more than six years for you to accumulate any capital if you do so, and it is not an easy road. Most people recognise this, and attempt to obtain capital before starting. Often they underestimate their requirements, because they do not have the skills to forecast adequately. So, how can you obtain this capital?

The safest, most constructive way is to use part of your savings. Look at a business in the same way as you do other investments: first assess the risk. In other words, think about what will happen if you lose all the money, and also how this might occur. Since there is a potential for loss, it is sensible not to put every last penny of your savings into a business unless you have a wealthy family who will bail you out.

EXAMPLE

This is a true story. Mike, Jim, David and Tom (not their real names) started a business in the late 1960s, using a total of £4,000 of their own savings. They were married men in their thirties, and had all worked successfully together in a large organisation, but they were frustrated with bureaucracy and wanted to 'go it alone'. In the late 1980s they sold the business to their managers (the company now employs over 200 people) and each received £3.5 million for their shares. At no time in the company's life did they ever borrow money, not even for a short-term overdraft, nor did they invest any more of their own savings. Each of them had interests outside the company

---

which they pursued actively. They were able to raise and educate their children, and fund various divorces, through their salaries as directors of their company. As the business expanded there was a need for more capital, and this came from the trading profits of the business – no dividends were paid on the shares.

This rigorous financial policy enabled the four men to become multi-millionaires. They chose to run the business without any borrowing because they were determined never to be answerable to a lender, which, they believed, was a way of losing control.

Contrast their attitude with that of the managers who bought out the business. The managers financed the purchase of Mike, Jim, David and Tom's shares through borrowing – they raised £14 million for this purpose – and at the same time borrowed more for expansion. At the time of writing, the managers are renegotiating their repayment schedule with the banks, a costly, time-consuming and potentially disastrous situation.

What did the four original directors do with their money? Two of them, Mike and Jim, were very successful in other fields as well, and had accumulated substantial sums from other sources. David bought a house in France and built a swimming pool at his London home (at current prices, these new investments are now worth less than they were in the 1980s). Tom had to pay a large part of his share to his ex-wife in a messy divorce soon after the sale. Jim has spent all of his share on luxury property and expensive living, but he has a large income from other businesses and other capital too. Mike didn't spend his share at all – he keeps it in conservative investments, and likes to spend some of the 'interest on the interest' on entertaining his large circle of family and friends who are rather in awe of him, especially as he is a quiet, unassuming old gentleman. As his wife often says, 'When we married, I never thought he would make any money.' Neither Mike nor his wife came from wealthy families; perhaps it was the experience of not having money early on that enabled them to achieve this level of prosperity.

Entrepreneurship as a career

Entrepreneurs come in all shapes and sizes – some have formal business educations from universities and business schools, while others have simply learned on the job. They can be of either sex, and are not of one distinct economic class or personality type; it is a myth that they are all brash go-getters, although many of them are. If there are any characteristics that they all seem to share, it is that they are 'survivors' who are able to learn from their mistakes, and that they truly enjoy the excitement of risk-taking.

A few people reading this book will have what it takes to become successful entrepreneurs, if not now, then at some time in the future. They probably know who they are. The majority of us would be better advised to concentrate on increasing our income through a career in employment, and developing our passive investing skills, which will ultimately result in prosperity. If this strikes you as an infuriating statement, perhaps you have what it takes to succeed in business!

Buying a franchise

This can be a lower risk route into the entrepreneurial world, and is often taken up by people with a military or large company background. It works like this.

- A company (the franchisor) has an established product or service.
- Private individuals (the franchisees) set up their own businesses using the franchisor's trade name, products and services.
- The franchisee finances his or her own business, and, in addition, pays the franchisor a one-off lump sum for the use of the trade name and the initial trading.
- The franchisor supplies the franchisee on an on-going basis, and takes a regular royalty from the franchisee's business income – this may be a percentage of sales, or included in the price of supplies.

Some of the best-known companies in the world are operated as franchises – did you know that Coca Cola and Holiday Inns are franchise operations? In their case, though, the franchisees must invest large capital sums, so that their franchises are often sold to large corporations, not private investors. Most franchises, however, are within the scope of smaller investors.

How much does it cost?

Few franchise companies have a fixed price for a franchise; usually, the price is set depending on the expected size of the outlet and its local market. You may be able to buy an outlet which is already running, in which case the price is likely to be higher. Franchisors are looking for people with good local knowledge, so it may be better not to move to another area in order to start an outlet. You can expect to pay a five-figure sum for a franchise.

True franchises are not pyramid schemes

Pyramid schemes (see page 36) are sometimes dressed up as franchises, but they are not the same thing. A true franchisor wants to see you succeed, not to take your money and run, so you will be able to get full information and proper professional advice before committing yourself. A good initial test is whether or not the product or service is well known and well established – if not, the franchise may not be a good deal.

Is franchising right for you?

The main benefit of buying a franchise rather than setting up on your own is that you have a known brand, probably with national coverage. This makes it easier to attract custom. If you haven't run a business before, it is an advantage that you get proper training and a realistic assessment of how much capital your business will require – a good franchisor will not let you start up if you do not have enough money to make the business work. If you are attracted by the idea, here are some basic questions to ask.

- Is the franchisor a member of the British Franchise Association (see Useful Addresses)?
- Can I visit several existing outlets?
- Is the royalty dependent on my success, or is it fixed? (The former is preferable.)
- How does the franchisor pick its franchisees?
- What happens when I want to terminate my contract? What restrictions are there on selling my business as a going concern?

The Enterprise Investment Scheme (EIS)

The EIS came in in 1994 as a tax incentive to encourage private investors to finance businesses. It succeeds the Business Enterprise Scheme (BES), a similar scheme which had attracted adverse criticism – it was claimed that the BES allowed certain types of investment which did not create employment.

The basic idea of the EIS is that it allows a private person to invest tax-effectively in new or expanding companies directly, while giving the business promoters the opportunity to raise capital at low cost. Investors must keep their money in the company for five years, and the scheme is of most interest to higher rate taxpayers. The social benefits of the scheme are alleged to include the potential for new job creation. The main rules of the EIS are:

- To qualify for the EIS, a company has to trade, rather than invest. Property, financial services and trading in financial securities and derivatives are generally excluded. The company has to continue to trade for a minimum of three years after raising the capital.
- 'Qualifying companies' can raise up to £1 million per fiscal year from their investors.
- The company must not be quoted on a stock exchange.
- The company can own other companies, but it cannot be owned itself by another company.
- New companies must start trading within two years of raising the capital.
- The rules allow investment funds to be created which invest in several EIS companies.
- A maximum of 50% of the company's assets can be in property (land and buildings).
- Companies don't have to be resident in the UK, but their main business must take place here.

The main thrust of these rules is to prevent one-off deals and investment in lucrative businesses which do not create much employment. There are also rules governing the investors themselves:

- The most you can invest in a single year is £100,000 and the minimum is £500. This money can be spread across several EIS companies.

- You must keep the investment for at least five years to qualify for tax relief.
- To get the tax relief you must be a UK taxpayer.
- Close relations of the directors of an EIS company, their business partners, employees and trustees are not allowed to invest.
- An investor can own a maximum of 30% of an EIS company.
- The investment must be in paid-up ordinary shares.
- If you and a relative who is not your spouse both invest, the money may be treated as a single investment for tax purposes.
- If you make a loss, it can be carried forward against capital gains in other years.
- You can become a director and earn fees if you were not connected with the company before you invested.

How the tax relief works

Investors get 20% relief on the amount they invest and any capital gains after five years are tax free. If you make a loss, you get relief at your current tax rate.

EXAMPLE

Tim is a higher-rate taxpayer (he pays 40% income tax). He puts £4,000 into an EIS company, and after a few years it goes into liquidation. Tim loses all his money. This is how he claims tax relief.

At the beginning:

Investment	4,000
Relief at 20%	800
Cost to Tim	3,200

Following his loss:

Total loss	3,200
Relief at 40%	1,280
Net loss	1,920

Although Tim invested a cash sum of £4,000, his total loss is only £1,920.

Suppose that Tim is luckier, and that the company breaks even after five years. His position would look like this.

At the beginning:

Investment	4,000
Relief at 20%	800
Cost to Tim	3,200

After he liquidates his investment:

Investment	3,200
Sale of shares	4,000
Tax-free profit	800

In this scenario, Tim makes an £800 profit even if the company only breaks even. It assumes, though, that Tim is able to sell his shares, which he may not be able to do if the company is only breaking even. Remember that unlike the better quality shares quoted on the stock market, shares in private companies generally have poor marketability.

Comment

If you are a higher rate taxpayer and have wide business experience, some EIS companies may possibly prove attractive. If you have never run a business yourself, you are in a similar position to the greenhorn who asks to be cut in to a poker game in a saloon in the Wild West. This type of investment does not offer the same level of protection to inexperienced investors as more conventional investments do.

Summary

The key points to think about if you want to become an entrepreneur are as follows.

- Running your own business is much harder work than being an employee.
- Most businesses have a negative cashflow for five or six years. Get a grounding in accountancy and financial forecasting.
- Businesses are vulnerable to red tape and bureaucracy. Plan for problems with officialdom!
- Recognise that you cannot trust business associates, and make contingency plans in case something goes wrong.

- If you use your own capital in the business, and finance expansion through retained profits, your business will not be vulnerable to the actions of lenders.
- Sell things and services that people actually want to buy.
- Avoid lawsuits. Remember the Romany curse, 'May you have a lawsuit and be in the right.' Don't expect justice in the courts.
- Be realistic about failure. If a business isn't working, cut your losses and get out. That way, you'll live to fight another day.
- Control the amount of credit you give. Issuing invoices is not the same thing as receiving the money!

13
TAX

Direct taxes become increasingly important as your net worth grows, because they are one of the main factors which inhibit that growth. As is the case in most other countries, the UK tax system is nightmarishly complicated when taken as a whole, so unless your financial situation is very straightforward, you would be well-advised to pay a professional adviser, preferably a chartered accountant, to help you handle your tax affairs. If your net worth is substantially more than, say, £200,000 or so, you may also need the services of a specialist tax lawyer to help plan your affairs tax effectively – they are not cheap, but may save you substantial amounts of tax.

In this chapter we look at:

- Who is liable to UK taxation?
- Tax avoidance versus tax evasion
- How UK residents are taxed
- Capital gains tax (CGT)
- Inheritance tax (IHT)
- The tax year
- Income tax
- Income tax rates for 1996/97

—— Who is liable to UK taxation? ——

This may seem a strange question – isn't everybody liable? – but it does depend on your circumstances, in particular your status with regard to:

- residence
- ordinary residence
- domicile

Residence

You may be regarded as being resident in the UK in any tax year in which you are present in the UK for at least part of that time. Anyone staying in the UK for at least six months in any tax year will always be regarded as being a UK resident for that tax year, and, depending on the individual's circumstances, the required period could be much less than six months.

Most other countries have similar rules to these, so it is possible for someone to be regarded as being resident in more than one country in any one tax year.

Ordinary residence

'Ordinary residence' is quite distinct from 'residence'. As it is the main criterion for capital gains tax (CGT), it is important to get the Inland Revenue to agree that you are 'not ordinarily resident' before you make a capital gain, if you want to avoid the tax. You can be resident in more than one country at the same time, but 'ordinarily resident' in only one country at a time.

Domicile

'Domicile' is quite distinct from 'residence' or 'ordinary residence'. If you are not domiciled in the UK, you are not liable for tax except on the money that you bring into the country. There are two kinds of domicile: domicile of origin and domicile of choice.

Your domicile of origin is usually the country where your father was domiciled when you were born. If you have a domicile of origin outside the UK, you may be able to live in the UK for a long time without ever having to pay UK tax.

Domicile of choice is harder to obtain. You have to be resident in a country and have 'the intention of permanent or indefinite residence' there to be domiciled in that country. If you want to change from a

UK domicile, you must intend never to return for anything more than brief, infrequent visits, or the Inland Revenue will deem that you haven't changed your domicile.

Each of these descriptions are used to assess whether or not you will be subject to UK taxation, or to the tax rules of another country, on:

- your earnings
- income from investments
- other sums of money, such as inheritance tax on death

– Tax avoidance versus tax evasion –

It can never be said often enough that it is all right to take steps to minimise your taxes, so long as you stay within the law.

- Tax avoidance means reducing or avoiding tax by using the rules to your best advantage, while keeping within the law.
- Tax evasion is the same thing – except that you break the law!

In a famous tax case in 1929, the judge, Lord Clyde, ruled that it is not wrong to arrange your financial affairs in such a way as to exploit the rules to your advantage, as long as you don't break the rules. This is the basis on which tax avoidance has been established as a perfectly legal activity in the UK. The legislation on tax is extremely complex and often unfair. There are many situations in which you cannot know for sure whether you are avoiding tax or evading it. Nevertheless you should make sure you use the very best adviser you can find, and do all that you can to stay within the law.

If you are not resident in the UK

If the Inland Revenue accepts that you are not resident in the UK for a period of time, you will not normally have to pay tax except on income arising in the UK. This means, for example, that people who work overseas for several years may not have to pay UK tax on the income that they earn abroad. If they are working in a country with no income tax, they may avoid income tax altogether.

The Inland Revenue apply several complicated tests to see if they think you are really not resident in the UK during any given period of time. You will need specialist help to establish your status in this regard.

What if I have close connections with other countries?

If you are not a UK national, or if you have a spouse who is not, get specialist advice from a tax lawyer. You may find that you are in a position to save tax.

—— How UK residents are taxed ——

Earned income

If you go to work abroad for a short period of time and earn money which is paid to you in that foreign country, then you could be liable not only to the tax of that country but also to UK tax. Most developed countries now operate what are called double taxation agreements which mean that one of the countries gives up its rights to tax the individual. Usually the country in which the work is done has the right to tax that income, and your country of residence gives up that right. For example, a UK resident who works for a short time in France will be taxed under French tax rules, and will not normally pay UK income tax on those earnings.

Unearned income

Unearned income is money you receive from investments such as stocks, shares, unit trusts, and rents on property you own. It may not seem 'unearned' to you, but that is what it is called.

If you have unearned income from investments held in another country which does not have a double taxation treaty with the UK, you could be taxed twice. Remember, though, that most developed countries do have double taxation treaties with each other. Suppose you received unearned income from investments in France. Because of the double taxation treaty between the UK and France, the foreign country (in this case France) will usually forego the right to tax the income, which will then be liable to UK taxation just as if that income had arisen in this country.

It is important to note that the taxation on income earned abroad by UK residents is paid when the income is earned or credited and not only when or if the money is returned to the UK.

———— Capital gains tax (CGT) ————

If you are a UK resident you are liable to CGT on gains made on the sale of assets wherever in the world they may be. The only exception is if you are domiciled in the Isle of Man or the Channel Islands. Trusts are also liable to CGT.

For example, if you own a villa in Italy which you sell at a profit then you may be liable to CGT in the UK on that gain. When you calculate the profit you made on the sale of an asset, you are allowed to take the inflation of the selling price into account.

What is CGT?

CGT was brought in in 1962, and extended in 1965. The rules have changed frequently, and no doubt they will change again in the future. Currently, the rules on CGT are so generous that many people in the City of London describe it as a 'voluntary tax'; this is because you can legally plan your finances in such a way as greatly to reduce CGT, or even to avoid it altogether. At present, the vast majority of capital gains that people make do not suffer any tax. At some periods in the past, however, CGT was far heavier – for instance, when people had to pay CGT on the profits from selling their main homes – so when you are making long-term financial commitments you should always consider the possibility of CGT becoming heavier.

What is the real difference between income and capital gains?

This is not always obvious, but the principle is that 'income' means your earnings, or profits on investments, which have some element of regularity. For example:

- interest earned on savings in a building society account
- salary from your job
- trading profits if you are self-employed

Capital gains are profits made on a 'one-off' basis, which are unlikely to recur and are not profits made in the ordinary course of employment or business, for example:

- profits on the sale of an antique
- profits on the sale of a second house
- profits on the sale of shares

In some cases, it is difficult to identify whether a profit will be liable to income tax or to CGT, and you should get specialist advice from an accountant.

The CGT rate

In the 1996/97 tax year, each person receives an annual exemption of £6,300. This means that you can make 'net chargeable gains' (the total of your chargeable gains minus your allowable losses) of up to £6,300 without having to pay CGT on them. If you are married, both you and your spouse get this allowance.

If your net chargeable gains exceed your allowance, you pay CGT at your highest marginal rate of income tax (see page 187). Thus, the CGT you pay could be 20%, 24% or 40% in 1996/97.

CGT exemptions and reliefs

There are currently quite a number of useful exemptions and reliefs. Here is a summary of the main ones.

- 'Chattels' (a name for personal possessions) which have a predictable life of less than 50 years are exempt from CGT. This means that things like cars, boats and caravans are normally exempt.
- Other chattels are exempt if you sell an item for £6,000. There also may be marginal relief (see page 187) if you sell an item for between £6,000 and £15,000.
- When you die, all your assets are revalued to their current market value free of CGT.
- In general, your main residence and any gilts or qualifying corporate bonds you own are exempt.
- If you retire after the age of 50, and you sell, among other things,

part or all of a business, or shares in a trading company in which you were a full-time working director or an employee, you are exempt of CGT, subject to various conditions, in particular that the chargeable gains are £250,000 or less. If the chargeable gains are between £250,000 and £1 million, you will only get half the exemption.

- If you retire before the age of 50 because of ill health, you may still be able to ge this relief.
- You may be able to defer CGT on gains you make by selling shares in a business, or sellings its assets.

Talk to your accountant about 'rollover relief' and 'holdover relief'.

Indexation

'Indexation' reduces CGT even further by letting you take inflation into account. Working this out can be tricky, especially since the Inland Revenue don't seem to want to hand out the tables you need to do the sums; however, the tables are published every so often in the *Investor's Chronicle*, and your accountant or tax adviser will be able to do the calculations for you.

EXAMPLE

Jim owns his own home in Manchester, where he lives and works, and a holiday cottage in Wales. He bought the cottage two years ago for £50,000, and has just been offered £60,000 for it, net of expenses. Jim's highest marginal income tax rate is 40%. How much CGT will he pay?

Since the cottage is a second home, Jim is liable for CGT if he sells it at a profit. Suppose inflation has only gone up by 3.3% in total during the two years he has owned the property:

Income from the sale	60,000
Purchase cost	50,000
Indexation	
(0.033 × 50,000)	1,650
Gain	8,350

Let's assume that Jim has made no other chargeable gains or allowable losses in this tax year. He deducts his allowance from the gain:

8,350 – 6,300 = 2,050,

and then he calculates the tax at his highest marginal rate of 40%:

40% of 2,050 = 820

Jim only pays £820 on his profit of £10,000.

CGT and shares

Most people won't have to worry about CGT much since their annual allowances will cover most gains. CGT can become a problem if you own shares, but remember that investments within a PEP are tax free, so CGT only affects shares you own outside a PEP. You might think that CGT only affects the very wealthy, but it can also hurt people who have come into, say, a six figure lump sum which they invest in the stock market – only a small part of such a sum can go into a PEP, so the rest of the portfolio could incur CGT on its gains.

A good way of reducing CGT on your shares is a technique called 'bed and breakfasting'.

Bed and breakfasting

When you 'bed and breakfast' you sell some shares on one day and buy them back on the next. It has the effect of 'crystallising' a capital gain or loss when you sell the shares, and when you have bought them back you have established a new 'base coat', or purchase price, for future CGT calculations. Here's how it works.

EXAMPLE

Sara has 5,000 shares in Megabucks plc. She reckons that they are good shares to hold for the long term, but the market has dipped, and they are presently worth less than she bought them for. If she 'bed and breakfasts', she can generate a loss

---

which can be carried forward against future capital gains which she may make on the shares, or on other investments.

	Purchased at	Bid price	Loss
5,000 Megabucks shares	5.00	4.20	£4,000

Let's assume that the purchase price includes the acquisition costs and has already been adjusted for indexation. 'Bed and breakfasting' will incur some costs. First, Sara sells the shares:

5,000 Megabucks sold at	4.20	21,000
Commission, say at 1.85%	388.50	
Administration, say	6.00	
Total received		20,605.50

Now she buys the shares back:

5,000 Megabucks bought at, say, 4.22		21,100
Commission, say	25	
Administration, say	6.00	
Stamp duty at 0.5%	105.50	
Total paid		21,236.50

Sara has actually had to pay out £21,236.50 − £20,605.50 = £631 in order to 'book' a CGT loss of £4,000 indefinitely into future years. If she is a higher rate taxpayer and she does make capital gains in the future, she will save 40% of £4,000, which is £1,600, less the cost of £631.

More points on bed and breakfasting

Dealing costs for bed and breakfasting vary, but are usually lower than for normal transactions. You must agree both the sale and the purchase with the same market maker, and settle both transactions on the same day. There is a small risk of the share price suddenly moving dramatically between the time you sell and the time you buy. If this happens you could lose money, but if you are bed and breakfasting large companies this risk is very low.

Inheritance tax (IHT)

Some people seem to think that it is wrong for people to inherit money. I am not one of them. If you are very rich indeed, then there may be a case for not passing on too much of your wealth to your children, since this can distort their characters – we've all heard about the 'poor little rich kids' who inherit fortunes and spend the rest of their lives in a misery of drink, drugs and broken relationships. If you find yourself in such a position as a parent, it seems to me that it is preferable for you to find an acceptable solution yourself, rather than let the government decide for you by taking all your wealth when you die.

For the rest of us, it makes sense to plan how to pass on our assets when we die. Currently, the IHT rules are fairly generous, so many estates (the legal term for your assets) will not attract much IHT. In 1996/97, the first £200,000 can be passed on to your beneficiaries free of IHT.

Make a will!

If you die without having made a will, you are said to have died 'intestate'. Intestacy is expensive to administrate, and in circumstances where there are no relatives with a legitimate claim to your estate, the money goes to the state.

Despite this, a very large number of people with substantial assets die intestate. There are many reasons why this happens, perhaps the most common being that a person has a superstitious feeling that making a will may somehow hasten death.

It is cheap to make a will. You can even buy a standard form or kit from newsagents that will do the job, so there is really no excuse for not taking action. In general, it is advisable to use a solicitor to draw up a will for you, especially if your financial affairs are at all complicated, because it is possible to make mistakes if you try the 'do-it-yourself' method. The solicitor's fee should be around £100.

Here are some important points to consider when making a will.

- Get professional advice on how to minimise IHT. Good tax planning can reduce the tax bill enormously. Every year or so, review your will with your adviser, and adjust it if your circumstances, or the tax laws, have changed.

- You must appoint people to be 'executors' of your will. An executor agrees to take responsibility for seeing that the legal formalities of dividing up your estate are done properly. In my view, you should never appoint a solicitor, bank, or other professional as an executor. This is because they tend to charge fees which are out of all proportion to the value of the work they do, and your relatives may be too upset to object. It is scandalous how often professionals dip their hands into estates in this way. Any responsible person can do the executor's job; if he or she needs a solicitor, then one can be engaged for specific matters at much less cost. It is a good idea to appoint at least two executors in case one dies, or cannot do the work.
- It is a good idea to think carefully about how you want the money to be divided. If you can leave everything to just one person, such as your spouse, you will reduce the chances of disputes.
- In case the people to whom you have left your estate (they are called the 'beneficiaries') die at the same time as you do – for instance in a car crash – it is wise to put some substitute beneficiaries in your will as well.

Tax planning and IHT

The current rules make it possible for people who are worth much more than the £200,000 which is free of IHT to avoid some or all IHT if they plan carefully with the help of professionals. You should be aware, though, that some gifts during your lifetime to people other than your spouse may be included in the £200,000 figure.

When there is an IHT liability, the amount can be considerable so it is very important for people with a high net worth to undertake financial planning in order to mitigate the liability to IHT, or at least to take out insurance policies to provide funds to pay IHT on their death. Remember that rich people are not popular with the general public! IHT rates have been much higher in the past, and it is always possible that they may become so again for political reasons.

The tax year

The tax year, or 'fiscal year', runs from the 6th of April in one year to the 5th of April in the next. Thus the 1996/97 tax year starts on 6 April 1996 and ends on 5 April 1997.

Most kinds of taxation are calculated on your income or gains within each fiscal year, and your residency or otherwise in the UK is taken in terms of each tax year. It is not possible to be counted as a UK resident for just three months – you either will or will not be deemed to be a UK resident for the whole of the tax year.

For income tax, your income will be calculated for the tax year, taking into account your personal allowances (see below) and the bands of income which are taxed at different rates (see page 187).

For capital gains tax, your gains in any one tax year are totalled when deciding if there will be any liability to pay CGT for that year.

Income tax

Personal allowances

Every UK resident is granted a personal allowance which means that a certain amount of income in each tax year will not be subject to tax.

The table below lists the more common personal income tax allowances. You will find the figures printed in many magazines and tax tables and usually in newspapers after the Chancellor of the Exchequer makes the annual budget statement ('the Budget'). The Chancellor usually changes personal allowances each year by increasing them roughly in line with inflation. You need to keep up to date with changes to these amounts.

Income tax allowances for 1996/97

Personal allowance	£3,765
Married couple's allowance	£1,790
Age allowance (ages 65–74)	£4,910
Married couple's allowance (age 65–74)	£3,115
Age allowance (75 or over)	£5,090
Married couple's allowance (aged 75 or over)	£3,155
Income limit for age allowance	£15,200
Widow's bereavement allowance	£1,790

Single person's and married couple's allowance

If you are unmarried and under 65, in 1996/97 the first £3,765 you earn will not be taxed. This is called the personal allowance.

If you are married, each spouse can earn up to £3,765 tax free. In addition, as a married couple you can earn a further £1,790 tax free. Since April 1993, at your choice, you can either have the married couple's allowance allocated to one of you, or it can be divided equally between both of you. Thus, if in any particular tax year you or your spouse has not earned enough income to use the part of the married couple's allowance allocated, it can be transferred to the other spouse. Relief on the married couples' allowance is 15% for 1996/97, so it is no longer a true deduction from income.

EXAMPLE

Jane and Adam are a married couple both aged 25. Adam earns £4,000 a year, and Jane earns £15,000 a year.

	Adam	Jane
Income	£4,000	£15,000
Less personal allowance	£3,765	£3,765
Subtotal	£235	£11,235

Now you can decide what to do with the married couples' allowance; in this case it would be sensible for Jane to claim the whole of the married couple's allowance, since Adam's tax liability is very small (20% of 235 = 47).

IMPORTANT

If you do not use the whole of your allowance in any particular year, the difference can **not** be carried forward to another year – you have lost it forever. For this reason, it is important to get your claim right.

Age allowances

You will see from the table of allowances on page 183 that there are large allowances for people aged between 64 and 74, and even larger ones if you are aged 75 or over. In addition, the married couples' allowances for older people are increased. The married couples allowance for those between 65 and 74 applies even if one partner is younger, and the same is true for those over 75.

EXAMPLE

Mr Smith is 54 and Mrs Smith is 67 in the tax year 1996/97. The allowances are initially as follows:

	Mr Smith	Mrs Smith
Personal allowances	£3,765	£4,910
Married couples' allowance	£3,115	

Mr Smith could claim all or part of the married couples' allowance. If the tax saving is greater by allocating the married couples' allowance to Mrs Smith, she can claim half or all of the basic (but not the age-related) married couples' allowance in any event.

Income limit for age allowance

In table of allowances you can see a figure for the income limit for the age allowance – this is £15,200 in 1996/97; if you are claiming the age allowances, (which are higher than the ordinary allowances for those under the age of 65) they will only be available in full if you have an income of £15,200 or less.

If you are over 65 with an income in excess of this level your allowance is reduced by £1 for every £2 by which the incomes exceeds £15,200.

EXAMPLE

Mr Brown is aged 76 and is single. His taxable income in 1996/97 is £15,800. What is his personal allowance?

Mr Brown will normally be entitled to the higher age allowance for a single person of £5,090, being over the age of 75. However, as his income exceeds the income limit for age

---

allowance by £600 (£15,800 less £15,200), his personal allowances will be reduced by half of this excess. The reduction to his personal allowances will be £300 (half of £600), making his revised figure for personal allowances £4,790 (£5,090 less £300).

If the rule had not existed, Mr Brown would have paid tax on all his income above his personal allowance of £5,090, which is £10,600 (£15,800 – £5,200). With this rule he will now pay tax on all of his income above his revised personal allowance of £4,790, which is £11,010 (£15,800 – £4,790).

Remember, though, that the age allowance can never be reduced below the ordinary allowance, however great the income. Thus, Mr Brown will always get a personal allowance of at least £3,765, however much his income increases. The same principle applies to married couples, with the above rule working to reduce the married couples' allowance, but only down to the standard rate of married couples' allowance, which is £1,790 in 1996/97.

Other allowances

There are a number of other personal allowances available in certain circumstances, the most common of which are:

- the additional personal allowance for children
- the widow's bereavement allowance

The additional personal allowance for children

This is claimed by single parents who are supporting children, in addition to their personal allowance. This effectively gives you the same total personal allowance as a married man. This extra allowance is a flat rate for a single parent regardless of the number of children you support. In 1996/97 it is £1,790.

The widow's bereavement allowance

This is an additional allowance granted, if you are a widow, in the tax year of your husband's death and in the following tax year. There is no similar allowance for husbands, although in the tax year of their wife's death they will still be granted the full married couples' allowance. This does not continue into the following year. Thus if the husband dies in August 1993, his estate (assets) would still be granted the full offset against his taxable income before his date of death.

His wife would also, in that year, get a personal allowance and the widow's bereavement allowance (which is equivalent to the married couples' allowance), increasing her total personal allowances. This also applies in the following tax year, but after that the additional allowance will cease.

If the widow has dependent children, she can also claim the additional personal relief for children. Relief on both of these allowances is 15% for 1996/97.

—— Income tax rates for 1996/97 ——

Taxable income	Rate	Total tax
(after deduction of allowances)		
First £3,900	20%	£780
Next £21,600	24%	£5,184
Over £25,500	40%	

The lower rate of tax

Suppose you are a single woman aged 25 with an income of £4,525 in 1996/97. How much tax will you pay?

1 Your personal allowance is £3,765. £4,525 – £3,765 = £760 taxable income.
2 The first £3,900 of taxable income is taxed at 20%. You have £760 of taxable income, so your tax will be £152.

The basic rate of tax

Suppose you are a single woman aged 25 with an income of £11,525 in 1996/97. How much tax will you pay?

1 Your personal allowance is £3,765. £11,525 – £3, 765 = £7,760 taxable income.

2 The first £3,900 of taxable income is taxed at 20% = £780.
3 The balance of your taxable income will be taxed at 24%: £7,760 – £3,900 = £3,860. 24% of £3,860 is £926.40.
4 Adding the results of 2 and 3 together, we get:

	Tax
£3,900 taxed at 20% =	£780
£3,860 taxed at 24% =	£926.40
£7,760 = total taxable income	£1,706.40 = total tax

On your income of £11,525 you must pay £1,706.40 income tax.

The higher rate of tax

Many people do not earn enough to be liable for tax in the 40% band (which is over £29,265 in 1996/97 for a single person). Let's suppose, though, that you are a single woman earning £32,525 in 1996/97. How much tax will you pay?

1 Your personal allowance is £3,765. £32,525 – £3,765 = £28,760 taxable income.
2 The first £3,900 of taxable income is taxed at 20% = £780.
3 The next £21,600 of your taxable income will be taxed at 24% = £5,184.
4 The balance of your taxable income will be taxed at 40%: this balance is £28,760 – (£3,900 + £21,600) = £3,260. 40% of £3,260 is £1,304.
5 Adding the results of 2, 3 and 4 together, we get:

£3,900 taxed at 20% =	£780
£21,600 taxed at 24% =	£5,184
£3,260 taxed at 40% =	£1,304
£28,760 = total taxable income	£7,268 = total tax

On your income of £32,525 you must pay £7,268 income tax.

Summary

These 'bands' of income tax rates, also known as 'marginal' rates, are a relatively new invention and are liable to change in the future. For this reason, it is important to stay alert and keep yourself informed about current and prospective changes. A bonus, a pay rise, or an unexpectedly successful investment can all push you over into a new band and, unless you plan for it, you could find yourself paying more income tax than you expected – get help from an accountant.

Self-assessment

The tax return system is currently changing to a 'self-assessment' system, which is supposed to be simpler – it is for the Inland Revenue, anyway. The first self-assessment returns will be sent out in April 1997; you have to fill in the figures yourself, and then either:

- send the form back by the end of September 1997 and let the Inland Revenue work out your assessment, or
- work out your own tax assessment and return the form by January 31st 1998.

The main difference with self-assessment is that taxpayers will be required to keep more records than they did before. From April 1996, you should start keeping such records as:

- P60, P160, P11D, P9D, P2 and P2K and P45 forms
- payslips and pay statements
- notes on tips and gratuities
- certificates for 'taxed award' schemes
- pension certificates and statements
- any details you have received from the Benefits Agency and the Employment Services Agency relating to state benefits and pensions
- bank and building society statements, cheque books and passbooks
- interest statements from other investments
- tax deduction certificates from your bank
- vouchers and statements relating to unit trusts you own
- all information on shares you buy, own or sell
- life insurance chargeable event certificates
- details of income you receive from a trust

In short, you must keep full records relating to any financial transactions or commitments. The Inland Revenue says that you only have to keep these records for 22 months after the end of the relevant tax year, but it would be wise to keep your records for much longer than this, especially if your financial affairs are complicated.

If you are self-employed, you already have to keep such records. The main change affecting you is that the self-assessment system is on a 'current year basis', so instead of paying tax on profits made in the year before the year of the tax return, you will pay tax on the profits arising in the tax year itself. 1996/97 will be a 'catch-up' year where an average of your profits will be taxed. You should discuss how to handle this with your accountant.

USEFUL ADDRESSES

American Stock Exchange
  (AMEX)
86 Trinity Place
New York, NY 10006
USA
Tel. 212 306 1000

Association of Investment Trust
  Companies (AITC)
Park House
16 Finsbury Circus
London EC2M 7DJ
Tel. 0171 588 5347

Bank of England
Gilt-edged and Money Markets
  Division
Bank of England
Threadneedle Street
London EC2R 8AH
Tel. 0171 601 4540

Financial Intermediaries, Managers
  and Brokers Regulatory
  Association (FIMBRA)
Hertsmere House
Hertsmere Road
London E14 4AB
Tel. 0171 538 8860

Investment Management
  Regulatory Organisation
  (IMRO)
Broadwalk House
5 Appold House
London EC2A 2LL
Tel. 0171 628 6022

Life Assurance and Unit Trust
  Regulatory Organisation
  (LAUTRO)
Centre Point
103 New Oxford Street
London WC1A 1QH
Tel. 0171 379 0444

The National Association of
  Citizen's Advice Bureaux
115–123 Pentonville Road
London N1 9LZ
Tel. 0171 823 2181

National Association of
  Securities Dealers (NASDAQ)
1735 K Street
Washington DC 20006
USA
Tel. 202 728 800

National Savings Stock Register
  (NSSR)
National Savings
Blackpool FY3 9YP
Tel. 01253 697333

New York Stock Exchange
  (NYSE)
Eleven Wall Street
New York, NY 1005
USA
Tel. 212 656 3000

Occupational Pensions Advisory
  Service (OPAS)
11 Belgrave Road
London SW1V 1RB
Tel. 0171 233 8080

Office of Fair Trading
Chancery House
53 Chancery Lane
London WC2A 1SP
Tel. 0171 242 2858

Personal Investment Authority
  (PIA)
3–4 Royal Exchange
London EC3V 3NL
Tel. 0171 929 0072

Securities and Investment Board
  (SEB)
Gavrelle House
2–14 Bunhill Row
London EC1Y 8RA
Tel. 0171 638 1240

Security and Futures Authority
  (SFA)
Cottons Centre
Cottons Lane
London SE1 2QB
Tel. 0171 378 9000

Stock Exchange
Throgmorton Street
London EC2N 1HP
Tel. 0171 588 2355

Unit Trust Association
65 Kingsway
London WC2B 6RD
Tel. 0171 831 0898

BIBLIOGRAPHY

Helen Baker, *Money Matters for Women*, Penguin 1993

Paul Delderfield, *Successful Borrowing and Coping with Debt*, Daily Telegraph Publications 1987

William Eng, *Trading Rules*, Pitman Publishing 1995

Leo Gough, *The Investor's Guide to Offshore Investment*, Financial Times/Pitman Publishing 1995

Leo Gough, *Teach Yourself Choosing a Pension*, Hodder & Stoughton 1996

Michael Joseph, *The Conveyancing Fraud*, Michael Joseph 1989

Bill Lubbock and Richard Stokes, *How to Get a Job*, Hamlyn 1989

C. Mackay, *Extraordinary Popular Delusions and the Madness of Crowds*, Harmony Books 1995

Harry Markowitz, *Portfolio Selection: Efficient Diversification of Investments*, Wiley 1959

Anthony Sampson, *The Money Lenders*, Hodder & Stoughton 1981

Fred Schwed Jr, *Where are the Customers' Yachts?*, Simon and Schuster 1940

Adam Smith, *The Money Game*, Random House 1968

George Soros, *The Alchemy of Finance*, Weidenfeld and Nicholson 1992

Michael Stolper, *Wealth: an Owner's Manual*, HarperBusiness 1992

Tolley's Tax Guide, Tolley Publishing Company, annual

John Train, *Preserving Capital and Making It Grow*, Penguin 1983

GLOSSARY

Advisory broker A stockbroker who advises clients on their investments as well as buying and selling on their behalf.
Annual charge Management fees levied on investments, often as a percentage of their value.
Arbitrage Taking advantage of the difference in price of the same product or rate in different places.
Arbitrageurs ('Arbs') Speculators who practise arbitrage, or buy shares in a company in the hope that it will be taken over.
Asset Anything which has a monetary value

Balance of payments The difference between the total value of money entering a country and the total leaving it in a year.
Balance sheet Statement of a company's financial situation at the end of the last financial year.
Bargain A transaction on the Stock Exchange
Basket currency An invented currency based on several national currencies such as the ECU and Special Drawing Rights.
Bear Someone who thinks the market will go down
Bearer bonds Bond certificates which can be held anonymously and used almost as freely as cash.
Bed and breakfast Selling shares and then buying them back to mitigate Capital Gains Tax.
Beneficial owner The true owner of a security, who may not be named in the register of ownership.
Bid price The price at which a unit-trust manager or market maker is willing to buy shares.

Blue chip   The top 100 or so companies on the stock market, reputedly stable investments.

Bond   Securities, usually paying a fixed rate of interest, which are sold by companies and governments.

Bonus issue   The issue of additional shares by a company to its shareholders at no cost; also called a 'scrip issue' or a 'capitalization issue'.

Bretton Woods   The place in New Hampshire, USA, where the post-war system of foreign exchange was agreed in 1944.

Call option   The right to buy shares at an agreed price within a certain time.

Capital Gains Tax (CGT)   A tax on the increase of value of assets realised in a particular year. In the UK, the threshold for capital gains below which no tax is payable is £6,300 for 1996/1997.

Capitalization   The total value at the market price of securities issued by a company, industry or market sector.

Chartist   Someone who studies charts in the hope of predicting changes in stock market prices.

Churning   Trading with a client's portfolio in order dishonestly to generate extra commissions.

Closed-end fund   A fund where the size of the total investment is fixed. All investment funds are closed-end.

Commodity   Any raw material.

Common stocks   The US name for ordinary shares.

Contract note   Written details of an agreement to buy or sell securities.

Conventional option   An option which is not traded.

Conventional stock/bonds   Bonds with fixed interest rates and repayment dates.

Coupon   The nominal interest rate on a fixed-interest security (bond), or a warrant which is detached from a bearer bond or bearer share certificate to be used to claim interest.

Currency hedging   Trying to reduce or eliminate exchange rate risks by buying forward, using financial futures or borrowing in the exposed currency.

Dealing costs   The cost of buying and selling shares; including the broker's commission, stamp duty and VAT.

Debenture   A bond issued by a company, paying a fixed rate of interest and usually secured on an asset.

Derivative An investment which is tied to an 'artificial' concept, like a stock index, rather than to stocks and shares themselves.

Designated terriroty The UK's Department of Trade and Industry (DTI) terms certain tax havens 'designated territories', meaning that they operate proper controls over their financial industries. They include the Isle of Man, Luxembourg, Jersey and Guernsey.

Devaluation The formal reduction in the value of a currency against others.

Dividend A regular payment out of profits by companies to their shareholders, currently taxed in the UK at 20%.

Domicile The country where you are resident for tax purposes; it is difficult, but not impossible, to change your domicile.

Double taxation treaty A treaty between countries to offset a person's tax liabilities in one country against those in another.

Earnings The net profit of a company, which is distributed to its shareholders.

EMS The European Monetary System is used by the EC to try to stabilise exchange rates between member states' currencies as a prelude to the introduction of a single common currency for Europe.

Eurobond A stock which is issued by a syndicate of banks and is usually bought and sold outside the country in whose currency it is denominated.

Eurocurrency Deposits of a currency which are held outside the country in which the money is denominated.

European Currency Unit (ECU) A basket currency of weighted amounts of the currencies of the EC countries.

Ex-dividend date The date when a holder of a UK bond receives the next interest payment.

Ex-dividend stock UK bonds which are sold to a buyer who does not receive the next due interest payment because the deadline for registration of the transfer has passed.

Exchange rate mechanism The system by which EC countries give a central rate against which their currencies' fluctuations are regulated.

Fixed assets A company's assets which are not being processed or bought and sold, such as buildings and machinery.

Flat yield Also called 'running yield' or 'interest yield', it is the income you earn in a year if you bought £100 market value of a bond. The figure is calculated by dividing the coupon by the market price and multiplying by 100.

Floating charge   A right to priority payment from the assets of a person or company.

Floating exchange rates   Currency exchange rates which change their rate according to the activity in the market.

Flotation   When a company first issues its shares on a stock exchange.

Forward exchange contract   An agreement to buy an amount of a currency at an agreed exchange rate on a fixed date.

FT Actuaries All-Share Index   A stock market index, divided into 40 sections, covering all shares quoted in the UK.

FT industrial ordinary share index   An index of the ordinary shares of 30 top companies.

FT-SE 100 index   The 'Footsie'; the principal index for the price of shares quoted on the London stock market.

FT-SE stocks   The 100 companies whose shares are represented in the FT-SE 100 Index. Generally regarded as blue-chip.

Fundamental analysis   Assessing the value of a share on a company's actual earnings, assets and dividends.

Futures   The right to buy or sell a financial instrument at an agreed price at some future time.

Gearing   The ratio between a company's share capital and its borrowings. High-gearing means a proportionately large amount of debt, and low-gearing means a small amount of debt.

Gilt-edged   Securities issued by the British Government, usually at a fixed interest rate. US gilts are called Treasury bonds.

Inflation   General increases in prices

Insider dealing   Trading in shares when in possession of price-sensitive information which is not known to the market. It is illegal to some degree in most markets.

Institutions   The large managed investment funds – including pension funds, insurance funds, unit and investment trusts – are known as institutional funds and are the major players in the stock market.

Investment bank   Called a 'merchant bank' in the UK, a bank which works as a financial intermediary, offering such services as take-over and merger assistance, and the placing of new share and bond issues.

Investment trust   A company which manages share portfolios, whose own shares are quoted on the stock exchange.

Junk bonds   Company bonds which are not rated by credit-rating agencies; they are 'low quality', and offer a higher rate of interest than other bonds.

LIFFE London International Financial Futures and Options Exchange

London Interbank Offered Rate (LIBOR) The rate of interest offered by commercial banks to other banks on the London interbank market.

Management charges Fees taken by fund managers to cover their overheads. They can be too high.

Marketability The degree of ease and speed with which a security can be sold.

Mututal funds The American name for unit trusts.

Net Asset Value (NAV) The net assets of a company divided by the number of shares it has issued gives the NAV per share.

Nominal value The value of a security printed on its certificate. Also called 'par' or 'face value'.

NSSR National Savings Stock Register.

Offer price The price at which a unit trust manager or market maker will sell a stock or share.

Open outcry Face-to-face trading where brokers shout their bids and offers out loud; used in most commodity and derivatives markets.

Open-ended A fund which has a variable amount of capital, and doesn't have to match its buyers with sellers.

Option The right to buy or sell a security at an agreed price within an agreed time span.

Ordinary share The most usual type of share, called 'ordinary' to distinguish it from other kinds, such as 'preference' shares which pay a fixed dividend.

Par value The nominal value of a share or bond, as stated on its certificate. This is not its market value.

Portfolio A collection of securities held by one investor or fund.

Preference shares Fixed dividend shares giving preference as a creditor over ordinary shareholders, but behind bond holders.

Price/earnings ratio (p/e) The market price of a share divided by its earnings (e.g. profits) gives the p/e ratio, which is the most commonly used measure of the 'value' of a share.

Put option The right to sell a security at an agreed price within an agreed time limit.

Quotation The price of a security currently fixed by a stock exchange market maker.

Rating Rating of bonds is done according to risk; the least risky bonds are rated AAA and the highest risk rated is D. Junk bonds are too risky to be rated.

Redemption yield Any one of several methods of calculating what interest rate is necessary for the market price of a bond to equal the net present value of the remaining interest payments and redemption value.

Reserve currency The currency which is most used by governments and institutions for holding cash reserves. Currently, it is the US dollar.

Rights issue When a company offers new shares pro rata to its own shareholders, usually at a discount.

RPI The Retail Prices Index.

Securities Any financial instrument traded on a stcok exchange, such as shares and bonds.

Self-regulating Organisations (SROs) Financial organisations which regulate, with varying degrees of effectiveness, the activities of their members.

Spread The difference between the prices of a share at which a market maker will buy (bid) and sell (offer).

Unit trusts UK savings schemes run by specialists for small investors; funds are invested in securities. In the USA they are called mutual funds.

Warrants Certificates, usually attached to bonds, which give the holder the right to buy shares at a given price and date.

INDEX